GARDEN PROJECTS

GARDEN PROJECTS

25 EASY-TO-BUILD WOOD STRUCTURES & ORNAMENTS

ROGER MARSHALL

The Countryman Press
Woodstock, Vermont

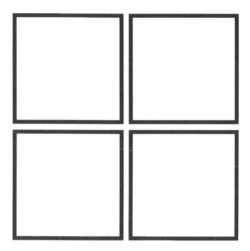

Illustrations by the author unless otherwise specified
Book design and composition by Charles Forsman

Published by The Countryman Press, P.O. Box 748, Woodstock, VT 05091
Distributed by W. W. Norton & Company, Inc., 500 Fifth Avenue, New York, NY 10110
Printed in the United States of America

CIP Data is available from the Library of Congress

Garden Projects
978-1-58157-211-7

10 9 8 7 6 5 4 3 2 1

CONTENTS

PREFACE

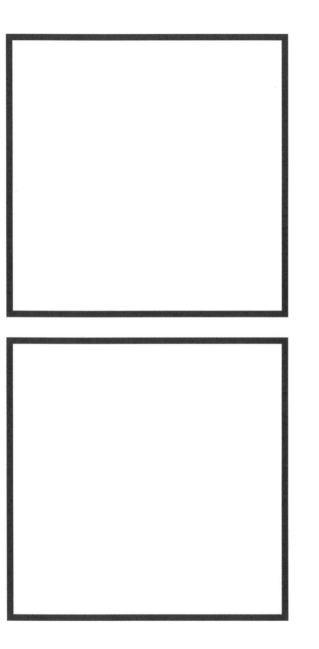

Back in 1980, I worked with a crew to build my own home. Since that time I have built a garage with my studio above it, two 300-square-foot greenhouses, cold frames, raised beds, and numerous other projects around the property. I also design boats for a living, and I have used that skill and the work on our property to develop this book.

The majority of these projects are fairly easy for a handy person, and they can be completed in a few hours with materials purchased from almost any hardware store. Others are more difficult and may take several days. A list of recommended tools accompanies each project description. Common woodworking tools such as sandpaper, paint, and paintbrushes may not be included in the lists, but it should be assumed that they will be needed for most, if not all, projects.

While most of these projects can be accomplished by one person, it should be said that no man is an island. I was not alone in the development of these projects. My son David and his friends made the gravestones in the Halloween project. Check them out, I'm sure you'll laugh long and loud. Also, over the years, I have found that any project, no matter how large or small, should not be started when the hardware store is closed. Scott and his crew at Jamestown Hardware were particularly helpful when it came to finding the right piece of material or particular screw for the job.

All of the drawings were modeled using Rhino software and rendered with Flamingo; both programs were developed by Robert McNeel and Associates. With these programs it is possible to develop the design and superimpose it on a digital photograph to better visualize the design. Steve Baker, another boat designer and Jamestown resident is the guru when it comes to using Rhino. When I got stuck, Steve spent an hour or three and bailed me out.

Roger Marshall
Jamestown, Rhode Island

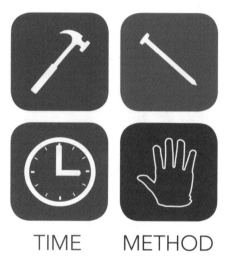

PROJECTS

PROJECT 1: MAKING A RAISED BED

One of the more efficient methods of gardening is to grow vegetables or flowers in a raised bed. Raised beds are easy to set up and easy to use, and best of all, you can build them without ever having to dig over the soil, if you so choose. Plus, you can adapt the raised bed to be a cold frame, a hooped bed, covered with glass, or just left open.

These raised beds took about 4 hours to build and are perfect for separating growing plants from walkways. To create deep soil, fill the beds with a mixture of manure, soil, sand, and compost.

 TIME   *About 4 hours*

⌐ TOOLS

Figure 1-1

» Hand saw or circular saw
» Light hammer for nailing
» Heavier sledgehammer for setting corner posts
» Square-ended spade or wide hoe to dig the trench for the bed walls
» 25' tape measure
» Garden twine

OPTIONAL TOOLS

» Portable drill and screwdriver bit

↖ MATERIALS

FOR A 4' X 12' BED

» Four 2" x 2" x 18" to 24" wooden posts with one end sharpened
» Two 2" x 10" x 12' wooden boards (You can also use 2" x 8" x 12' boards)

Two 2" x 10" x 4' boards
(You can also use 2" x 8" x 4' boards)

» Fasteners: 2 1/2" or 3" exterior-grade galvanized or ceramic-coated screws, or 16d nails

✋ METHOD

STEP ❶

Determine the size of your growing bed. The width of your growing bed is critical to ease of use. A 4'-wide bed is the maximum recommended size, as you will have easy access from both sides. If you can only reach in from one side, make it a 3'-wide or even a 2'-wide bed. If you build it wider than this, you will have to walk on the bed, which will compact the soil and make it more difficult for plant roots to spread and gain necessary moisture and nutrients.

As for length, you can make your growing bed as long as you want. The longest lengths of lumber commonly available are 16'. If you want to build a longer bed than this, you can buy longer pieces at some lumber yards, or you can butt the ends of smaller pieces together. For example, some of my growing beds are 44' long, but none are wider than 4'. For this example, we will assume the bed is to be 12' long x 4' wide.

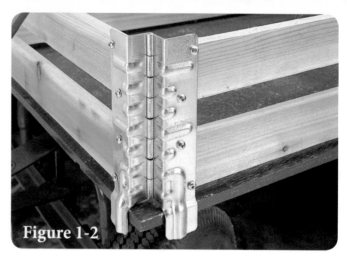

Figure 1-2

STEP ❷

Find the right location. It is best to site your growing beds in an east-west orientation. This way, if you put a tall tomato plant on the north side of the bed, it will not shade any plants behind it.

Ideally, the ground should be flat to make it easy to set up and tend your growing beds. If your ground is sloped, site the beds on the most southerly facing side possible, as long as the slope is not too steep. You can step your beds along the slope to get the maximum amount of sunlight to each bed. Building a raised bed on the north side of a building or hill is to be avoided.

STEP ❸

Measure the bed area. You will need a measuring tape and four (more if the bed is to be long) 2" x 2" x 18" to 24" sharpened posts. (You can cut your own 2" x 2" posts from 2" x 4" boards, as in Figure 1-1, or you can use metal corners, as in Figure 1-2, in place of the wooden posts.) Your posts can be made of cedar, regular pine, or any other kind of durable wood. I prefer not to use pressure-treated lumber in the vegetable garden simply because I do not want the chemicals used to treat the wood leaching into the soil around plants that I am going to eat.

If we are going to lay out a bed from east to west, the first step is to hammer a post a few inches into the ground at the bed's northwest corner. Measure 3' 9" south and hammer in a second post to form the west side of the bed. (Because dimensional lumber measures 1 1/2" wide for a 2" board, the length of the bed side is reduced from 4' to 3' 9" by the thickness of the 2" by 10" planks used to form the sides of the bed.) Now measure the bed length by extending your tape measure 12' to the east. Mark the spot and hammer in another post. Now complete the square to the northeast corner by measuring 3' 9" north and hammering in your final post at that point. Figure 1-3 shows an exploded view of the raised bed; the four corner posts are hammered into the ground, and the lumber is cut to length.

Figure 1-3

STEP 4

Square the bed. Now comes a critical step. Measure the length of the two diagonals from opposite corners. If they are the same length then your bed is square. If they are uneven, you should adjust the location of your stakes until the bed is square.

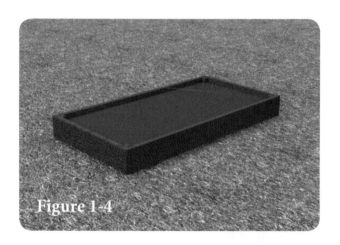

Figure 1-4

STEP 5

Assess the bed size. Run a length of string around the corner posts to give yourself a sense of the finished size. Is it large enough for your needs? Can you reach across the bed comfortably?

STEP 6

Build the frame. The next job is to screw or nail 2" x 10" x 12' (51 mm x 250 mm x 3.7 m) boards to the posts. I prefer to screw the boards in place; this makes it easier to remove them should I decide to modify the bed. Also, the impact of hammering nails into the sides and posts might knock them out of true. Use 2-1/2" ceramic-coated screws for longevity. Sheetrock screws will rust away in four or five years. The 12'-long boards are screwed to the outside of the posts on the north and south sides. Because you hammered in the posts at 3' 9", the 4' boards at the east and west sides will overlap the posts and the end of the 12' planks. With the ends in place, the frame is complete.

STEP 7

Prepare the ground. Now you can either dig the area of the bed over by hand or rototill it. (If you plan on rototilling, do so before you put one end of the bed frame in place.) This will loosen the soil below the new soil you create in order to foster good drainage and root growth.

STEP ⑧

Fill your growing bed. Now that your growing bed is set in place, it is time to create good soil in which to grow your plants. To do this, I recommend a technique known as sheet composting. First, to reduce weeds, lay several sheets of black-and-white newspaper or cardboard over the soil. (Newspaper and cardboard are made from tree pulp and will rot away. Do not use colored newsprint; it may contain heavy metals in the ink.) Next, put a 2" to 3" layer of brown leaves over the newspaper. Then put a 2" layer of green grass clippings on top of the leaves.

The idea is to build layers of green (high nitrogen) and brown (high carbon) materials. Green materials are: dried blood, horse manure, grass clippings (from untreated grass only), chicken manure, feathers, fish wastes, and seaweed. Brown materials are: wood ashes, hay (though hay tends to be full of weed seeds), straw, brown leaves, cow manure, greensand, and kitchen (non-meat) wastes. Build these layers until your raised bed is piled high above the side boards. In two to three months, all these materials will have rotted down to about half their height. Dig over the bed to thoroughly mix the materials. Dig over the bed again monthly to ensure everything is well mixed, and in five to six months you can start planting vegetables and flowers into your new bed.

Of course, if you do not want to wait that long, you can simply fill the bed with well-rotted compost and soil in about equal quantities to the top of the planks (as shown in Figure 1-4) and plant immediately.

↱ OPTIONS

With your raised bed in place, there are a number of different types of row covers that can easily be added to help extend your growing season or to keep animals and insects off your crops. Figure 1-5 shows these various row cover designs you can build over a raised bed:

(A) spun fleece cover over hoops made from plastic water pipes

(B) glass cloche using recycled pieces of glass

(C) cold frame using storm windows

If you decide to build a cold frame, make the corner posts as long as your cold frame is high at the back and front. For example, for a 4' wide bed using 5' long panes of glass, the back wall will be 3' high. You can also make the cold frame removable by making the stakes half the height of the side boards and allowing the corner stakes of the cold frame to fit on top of the raised bed stakes.

✳ SPUN FLEECE COVER ✳

The easiest method is to attach a frame to the bed over which is hung a protective fabric cover. This will help keep predatory insects off your crop and hide it somewhat from larger predators. You can also lay the fabric directly over the growing bed, but I have found that it flaps in the wind and damages smaller plants.

To make this cover, use six 1/2" or 3/4" x 10' sections of plastic water pipe. Half-inch pipe is easier to bend but not as rigid as the 3/4" pipe. If you warm it slightly, the more rigid pipe is easier to bend. *(Wear safety glasses; the plastic pipe sometimes snaps!)* The six pieces of pipe will form half-hoops across the width of and spaced evenly along the bed. Use 1/2" or 3/4" pipe clamps screwed to the sides of the bed to hold the pipe. Push one end of each pipe into the ground inside the frame on each side of the bed. Then drape your 10'-wide x 12'-long (depending upon the length of your bed) spun fleece, other fabric, or plastic sheet over the frame. Putting the pipe inside the growing bed allows the fleece to hang over the wooden structure. Then use furring strips to screw the fleece to the wooden frame.

✳ GLASS CLOCHE ✳

Another option for covering the raised bed is to use panes of glass leaned together to form a triangle with the bed and held together at the top by a specially made wooden clip. I use 30" x 18" panes of glass placed horizontally with the bottoms placed about 24" apart. The tops are held together to form a triangle with a specially cut wooden block (see Figure 1-5). (You can also purchase cloche clips from some suppliers.) I find that two blocks are needed to hold 30"-long glass panels. I also have two 66"-long panels that are held with three clips, but these take two people to position them properly.

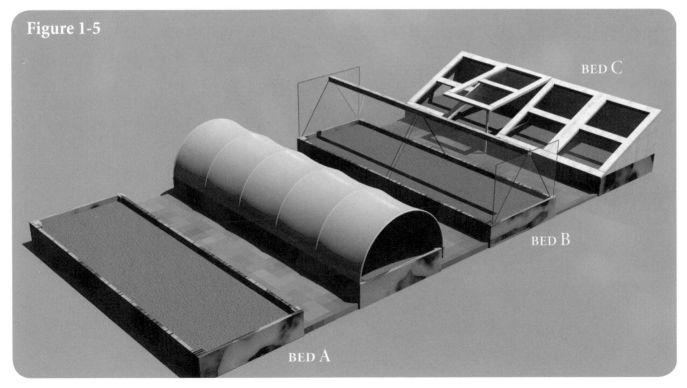

Figure 1-5

BED C

BED B

BED A

✴ COLD FRAME ✴

I was given a few old storm windows 5' long and decided that they would make a perfect cold-frame cover for my raised bed. With my 4' wide bed and 5' windows, I cut new 2" x 2" x 3' posts and a 3' x 12' plywood panel for the back wall. A frame for the windows made up the sloping front, while two triangular boards closed up the sides of the frame. (See Project 16 for more on the cold frame.) You can also make the cold frame removable by making the stakes half the height of the side boards and allowing the corner stakes of the cold frame to fit on top of the raised bed stakes.

✴ TALL RAISED BED ✴

Many people with physical disabilities cannot easily reach down to a 10" tall raised bed. A more accessible bed will need to be much higher—up to 3' in some cases. You can make a bed of this size by using the same techniques as in steps 1 through 5, but your posts will need to be 5' long and the sides will be made from 4" x 4" or 6" x 6" planking. The bed can then be filled as in Step 7. Figure 1-6 shows how the raised bed can be elevated for the handicapped gardener.

Figure 1-6

PROJECT 2: A SIMPLE COMPOST BIN

This single bay compost bin is extremely simple to make and to use.

If you want to make compost from vegetable kitchen scraps, lawn clippings, and debris from a small garden, this compost bin is very simple and easy to make. It is 3' square, stands 3' high, and is wrapped with 1" or larger mesh chicken wire. The gate can be made of scrap lumber and hinged on one side. (You can also tie it in place, if you don't want to add hinges.)

🕐 TIME

About 6 hours (about 4 hours with a helper)

⚒ TOOLS

- » Hand saw
- » Heavy sledgehammer to pound in the posts
- » Wire cutters
- » Staple gun

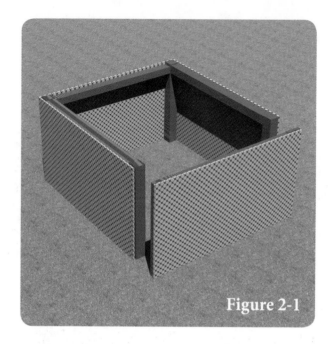

Figure 2-1

MATERIALS

For One Bin

- » Four 2" x 4" x 4' 6" (or 4" x 4" x 4' 6") stakes
- » One 3' x 9' x 1" section of mesh chicken wire
- » One 3' x 4' x 1" section of mesh chicken wire

For Gate

- » Four 1" x 3" x 3' boards with lap joint at each corner

Fasteners:

- » 1/2" or longer staples

✋ METHOD

This compost bin is intended to be simple to construct and to enable the compost to be turned three or four times before it is ready for use. Making the gate removable allows easy access to the contents.

STEP ❶

Mark out the area for your bin. This one is designed to be 3' x 3', but if you have a lot of leaves and lawn clippings, you can make it 4' x 4' or even larger. Hammer the corner posts into the ground to a depth of 18"; any shallower and the sides may bow outwards from the weight of the compost. Check that the bin's footprint is square, but an inch or so off will not matter.

STEP ❷

Staple the long length of chicken wire to one of the gate posts. Make sure that the bottom of the wire is at ground level. (You can dig a small trench if you like and bury the wire a few inches, but I find that this will corrode the chicken wire more quickly.)

STEP ❸

Work your way around the bin, keeping the wire taut, and staple it in place at each post until you end up at the opposite gate post. If you wish, you can screw a thin 1" x 2" x 36" slat over the wire at each gate post to help hold it in place. Figure 2-1 shows the bin with wire around it. To stop the bed from bulging when it is full, you can screw or nail wood slats across the top of the chicken wire from post to post and staple the wire to them.

Tip: Fill your bed in layers using both brown and green compost materials as explained in Poject 1. Pile the materials higher than the sides of the bed and let them rot down. I find that the bed heats up to about 150 degrees F and cools down after about six weeks. When it has cooled, turn the compost into the next bay. It will heat up to about 120 degrees F. When it has cooled, turn it back into the original bay. Ideally, you will turn your compost up to five times. I then screen the compost and use it on my garden beds.

STEP ❹

Build the gate. This is constructed from the 1" x 3" lumber with a lap joint at each corner. Glue and screw it together into a frame, making sure that it is square. When the glue is dry, staple the 3' x 4' section of chicken wire on the inside of the gate, or you can staple the chicken wire to the outside. By putting it inside, it will be forced against the gate as the bin fills and will not try to pull off the staples.

STEP ❺

You can hinge the gate using two 3" hinges on one side and a simple hook and clasp on the other side. An alternative is to install four hook-and-eye latches on each corner of the gate, with the hooks on the gate and the eyes on the compost bin. Or you can simply put the gate inside the posts and let the weight of the compost make it lean against the post. However, that might make it difficult to remove the gate when the bin is full.

3-bay compost bin

OPTIONS

MATERIALS

FOR A THREE-BIN SYSTEM

- » Eight 4" x 4" x 4' 6" posts, one end sharpened
- » Ten 2" x 4" x 4' cross braces
- » One 4' x 28' x 2" mesh chicken wire or hardware cloth section
- » Three 4' x 4' x 2" mesh chicken wire or hardware cloth sections for gates

FASTENERS:

- » 3" exterior-grade screws to hold the cross braces, 1" staples to hold the chicken wire in place

TIME *About 4 to 6 hours*

METHOD

If you make a lot of compost, one small bin is not going to allow you to turn the compost and let it rot properly. A three-bay compost bin is an essential tool in creating a wonderful garden. This three-bay bin is made like a single-bay bin, with stakes hammered into the ground and wrapped with chicken wire or hardware mesh. Because the bays may be filled far higher than the single compost bin, the posts are reinforced with a top brace to make the entire unit sturdier.

When using this bin, fill one of the side bays (bay 1) first. When it is filled with compost, turn the entire load into the center bay (bay 2). This has the effect of putting the oldest compost on top and encouraging it to rot better. After about six weeks, move the compost in bay 2 into bay 3 while bay 1 is being filled with fresh material. In another six weeks, turn bay 3 back into bay 2. Six weeks later, turn bay 2 into bay 3 again. This process should result in compost ready to be used. At this time, turn bay 1 into the bay 2.

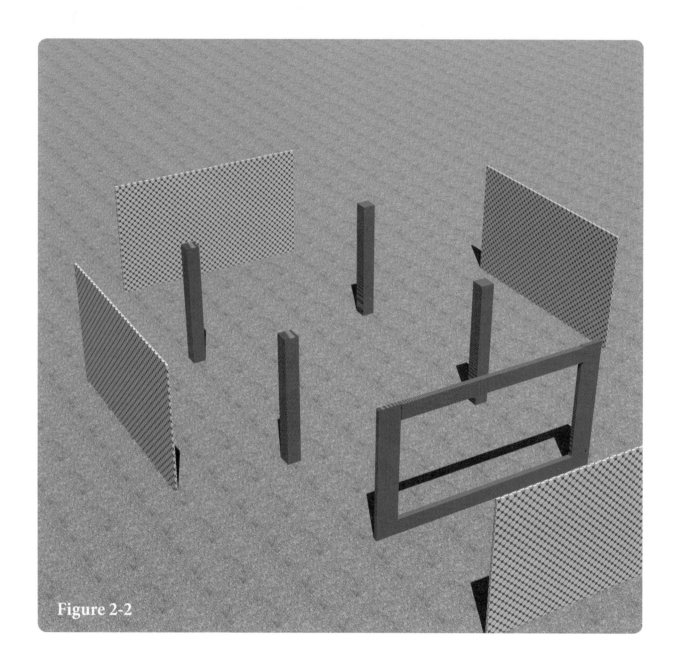

Figure 2-2

PROJECT 3: A LIVING PLANT WALL

A living plant wall can be used as an attractive screen to divide or hide many areas. It is relatively easy to make with plant pots positioned at a 45-degree angle. (If you slope the pots any farther, they become difficult to water.) One of the benefits of this type of system is that you can build in a drip irrigation system to make watering easier. This wall is 5' high by 4' wide, but you can make your wall any height or width that can carry the weight of the plant pots. The shelves can be supported by cleats or fitted into routed grooves in the side boards (in which case, eliminate the cleat wood from the materials list).

This plant wall can hold pots of green plants or flowers to make an interesting divider in the garden or on a patio.

⚒ TOOLS

» Circular or table saw

» Screwdriver

» Cordless drill

OPTIONAL TOOLS

» Router

⟍ MATERIALS

FOR THE WALL

» Two 1" x 8" x 5' boards for the sides

» Four 1" x 6" x 4' boards for the shelves

» Four 1" x 2" x 4' or 1" x 3" x 4' boards for the shelf stops

» Four 1" x 2" x 6" boards for front shelf cleats

» Four 1" x 2" x 2" or 3" boards for back shelf cleats

» 1 1/4" galvanized or ceramic-coated exterior screws as fasteners

FOR THE BASE

» One 1/2" x 10" x 5' piece of plywood

» Two 1" x 2" x 5' boards

» Two 1" x 2" x 8-1/2" boards

» 1 1/2" galvanized or ceramic-coated exterior screws as fasteners

» One plastic sheet or tray to line the base to keep water in. (You can also have a copper tray made to fit the base. Adding pebbles to the tray hides the water level and raises the humidity.) The tray can also be raised off the floor by installing it on additional 1" x 2" x 8 1/2" supports placed 3" in from the ends.

⏱ TIME *4 to 6 hours*

✋ METHOD

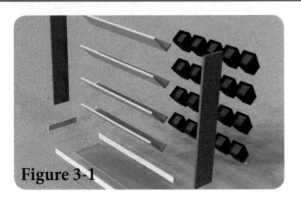

Figure 3-1

STEP ❶

Cut all the wood to size as listed in the materials sidebar. Figure 3-1 shows an exploded view of the wall to show where the parts go.

STEP ❷

Make up the shelves first by drilling and screwing the stops to the shelves. The shelf stops also serve to give the shelves some rigidity to prevent sagging when bearing the weight of the filled plant pots. Figure 3-2 shows a shelf unit fully assembled.

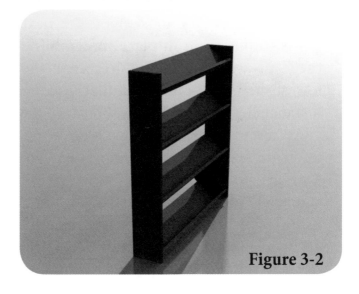

Figure 3-2

Tip: You can change plant pots as often as you wish. For example, you might have all pansies in spring and change them to marigolds or carnations in summer to give more color to your living wall. You can also grow vines in the top two rows and let them hang down to cover the lower part instead of installing additional pots.

STEP ❸

Install shelf supports. If you plan to use cleats to support your shelves, the next job is to put them in place. Assembling the unit with cleats requires that the lowest shelf be installed first (because the distance between shelves is too small for your screwdriver), and that you work upwards, screwing and gluing as you go. Measure and mark the location on the side walls of the top of each shelf. Then using a carpenter's square, mark a 6", 45-degree line on the side wall. Screw the cleats to the upright sections as shown in Figure 3-3, then screw the shelf to the top of the cleat, so the top of the shelves line up with the front edge of the unit. If you would prefer that the screw heads do not show, you can screw the cleat into the shelf (in which case you will need to start with the top shelf).

If you plan to install the shelves into grooves routed in the side walls, rout out a half-inch wide groove in which to install the shelves as shown in Figure 3-4. Set the side wall on the bench or on the ground and glue the shelves (with front support in place) in each slot. Take the other sidewall and lay it over the upright shelves. Align the shelves and glue them into place. You can screw the top sidewall to the shelves if desired. Check to see that the unit is square by measuring the

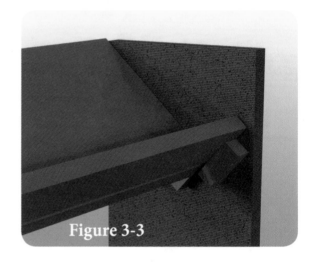

Figure 3-3

diagonals. Leave the glue to set before turning the unit over and screwing the other ends of the shelves in place. Stand the unit upright while you make the base. Figure 3-4 shows the unit at this point.

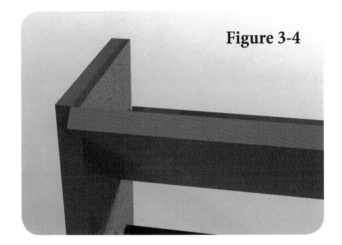

Figure 3-4

STEP ❺

Install the plant pots on the shelves as shown in Figure 3-6. It is easiest to water the pots while they are upright, and you might want to remove each plant to water it before replacing it on the shelf.

STEP ❹

Assemble the base by screwing through the base into the sidepieces. If you use a plastic liner, you might want to add 3/4" x 1/4" trim strips around the top edges of the base to hide the liner edges as shown in Figure 3-5. Set the upright shelves on the liner and fill the base around the shelves with small stones or pebbles.

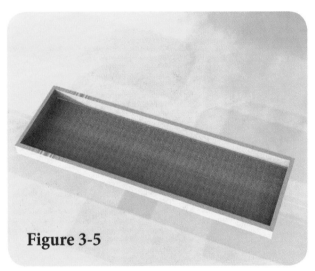

Figure 3-5

↱ OPTIONS

You can make the plant shelves almost any length up to about 4 feet and stack them up to six high. You should not go higher than five or six shelves without bracing the plant wall in some manner to prevent it from falling over. If the unit were to be made with six or eight shelves high, It should be fastened to a wall by screwing through one side directly into a previously located stud in the wall.

Figure 3-6

The finished trolley. (I had a scrap 2" x 8" board, so I used it for the middle section.)

Suppose you have a large houseplant that needs repotting. How do you get it outside to repot? If you lift it and carry it, there could be a visit to a chiropractor in your future. This pot trolley is intended for moving large plants across any reasonably flat surface. It is made quickly and simply using four casters purchased at any hardware store (if your terrain is uneven, buy larger wheels), and several pieces of scrap 2" x 4" lumber.

⚒ TOOLS

» Handsaw or circular saw
» Cordless drill with 3/16" drill bit (for screw holes), and Phillips head bit to suit screw heads

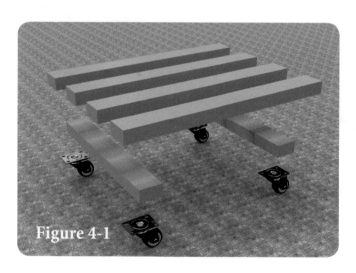

Figure 4-1

\MATERIALS

» Four 2" x 4" x 18" boards
» One 2" x 8" x 18" or two 2" x 4" x 18" boards
» Four 3"-diameter castors. (Use a larger size for rolling on rough surfaces. For rolling on smooth indoor surfaces, they can be 2" diameter.)

FASTENERS:

» Sixteen 2-1/2" to 3" screws and twelve 1/4" x 1-1/4" screws (Ceramic-coated screws are best, but slightly more expensive than sheetrock screws.)
» You will also need three or four screws per castors sized to suit the castors you will use.

🕐 TIME   *About 1 hour*

✋ METHOD

STEP ❶

Assemble the pieces cut to length as shown in Figure 4-1, an exploded view of the trolley (with four 3"-diameter castors below).

STEP ❷

Screw the cross braces to the longitudinal pieces using 2 1/2" screws. You can obtain a neater look by screwing upwards through the cross braces. Check that the work is square before screwing everything together. Figure 4-2 shows the cross braces screwed to the longitudinal pieces.

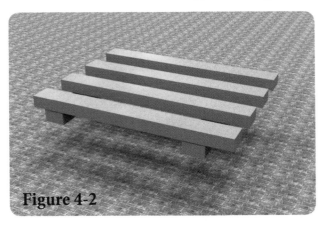

Figure 4-2

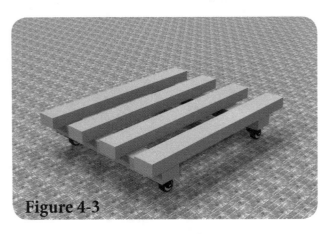

Figure 4-3

STEP ❸

Set the castors in place and drill 1/8" holes for the 1/4" screws. Screw the castors in place and turn the plant trolley over. It is now ready for use. Figure 4-3 shows the trolley fully assembled. If you want to be sure the trolley does not damage your pots, you can nail or staple a piece of old carpet over each longitudinal.

Lattice fencing can be purchased in a variety of sizes and materials—pressure-treated and non-pressure-treated wood, or white, brown, and green plastic. Neither material is very expensive, and it can be used for many projects, including fencing or in the garden, for supporting grape vines, tomatoes, beans, peas, or flowering vines. If you wish you can even use it to make a pen for small to medium animals, although animals the size of cattle and horses might break through rather easily.

 TIME

About 1 hour to build one section of lattice fence

↗ TOOLS

- » Handsaw or circular saw
- » Hammer
- » Screwdriver
- » Tape measure

MATERIALS

FOR ONE 8' SECTION OF FENCE OR SUPPORT.

» Two 4" x 4" pressure-treated posts of a suitable length. Eight-foot-long posts are usually the smallest that you can buy. They can be buried up to 3' deep (if you want to dig a hole that deep!) and cut off at the correct height.

» Two 2" x 4" x 8' boards for top and bottom support

» One 2' x 8' or 4' x 8' section of lattice (depending upon the height of fence you are building)

» Caps and finials for the 4"x4" posts

» U-shaped channel (use extruded channel for plastic trellis) for edging the trellis

» Two 1" x 2" pine boards nailed and glued 1/2" apart around the frame to make the U-shaped channel. (Use 3" galvanized or ceramic coated finish nails to fasten the pine boards to the 2" x 4".)

» Nails: 2" flat-head nails (set in the bottom of the U-shaped channel to fasten it to the 2" x 4".)

» Screws: 6" or 8" TimberLOK screws (to fasten the top and bottom rails into the uprights)

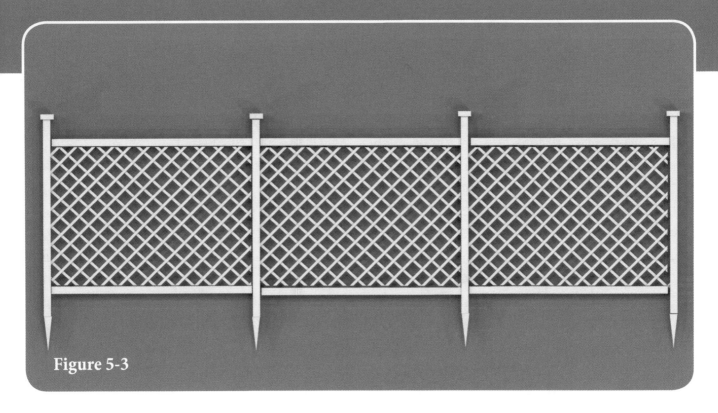

Figure 5-3

MATERIALS NOTES: TO BUILD ONE 8'-LONG SECTION OF FENCE YOU WILL NEED TWO 4" X 4" PRESSURE-TREATED POSTS, CUT TO MATCH THE HEIGHT OF YOUR FENCE; A 2" X 4" BOTTOM RAIL; AND A CAP RAIL OF SOME FORM. I USED A 2" X 4" BOARD AS THE CAP RAIL, BUT YOU CAN ALSO USE BALUSTER RAILS, 1" OR 2" X 3" OR 4" MAHOGANY OR OTHER MATERIAL AS A CAP RAIL.

YOU CAN BUILD THREE OR FOUR SECTIONS OF FENCE WHILE IT IS LYING ON THE GROUND, BUT YOU WILL HAVE DIFFICULTY RAISING THE COMPLETE UNIT AND SETTING IT IN PLACE. THE BEST WAY TO BUILD AN ENTIRE FENCE IS TO BUILD IT ON THE GROUND AS SHOWN IN FIGURE 5-3, THEN TAKE IT APART AND SET THE FENCE POSTS IN THEIR HOLES. THEN BUILD THE SECTIONS IN BETWEEN THE POSTS.

✋ METHOD

STEP ❶

Dig your post holes. The depth of each hole should be at least one quarter to one third of the fence height. Set the post in the hole and plumb to ensure it is vertical on all sides. Check that the second hole is exactly 8' from the first if you plan on butting lattice to the post. You may have to brace the posts to ensure that they do not move.

STEP ❷

Mark the height of the bottom rail. Before settling on the total fence height, check around the area that you are fencing in, to ensure that you will not need to change the rail height at a later time. Nothing detracts more from the symmetry of a fence than an inadvertent change in height, especially if you have to change back to the original level later.

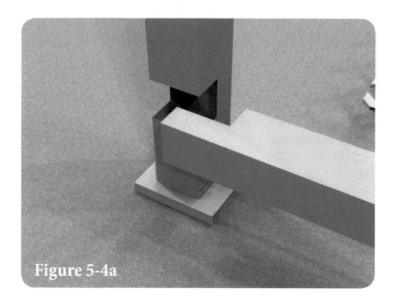

Figure 5-4a

STEP ❸

With the height marked, cut lap joints as illustrated in Figures 5-4a and 5-4b. Set your rotary saw to cut half the thickness of the post. Mark off the width of the lap joint the correct size to accept the bottom 2" x 4" rail and use your rotary saw to cut a series of slots about 1/2" apart between those marks. Use a chisel to clean out the remaining wood, ensuring the joint is no deeper than half the thickness of the wood. Then cut a notch in the rail end half the width of the rail and the length equal to the post width. If you use this lap joint method at the bottom rail/post joint, you will have to trim the lattice to fit because the lap joints will shorten the top and bottom rails by about 3 1/2" on each end, for a total of 7" per rail.

If you do not want to cut a lap joint, you can fasten lumber up to 4" x 4" with 6" or 8" TimberLOK screws. This is not as strong as a lap joint in that all the strength is in the thickness of the screws which may corrode over time.

Figure 5-4b

STEP ❹

Screw or nail the U-shaped channel pieces to the bottom rail (for plastic lattice) or nail (use 2 1/2" [8d] finish nails) two 1" x 2" pine strips, spaced 1/2" apart (for wood lattice) along the length of the rail. The simplest method of installing the U-shaped bottom rail is to screw it to the supports. (If using the lap-joint method, the channel will have be miter cut 3 1/2" shorter at each end, at the start of the lap joint.)

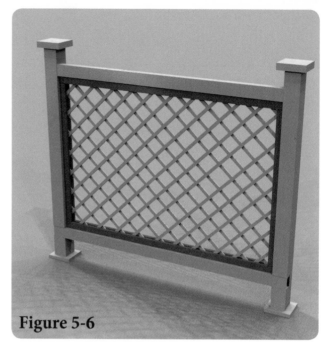

Figure 5-6

Figure 5-5

STEP ❺

Install the vertical U-shaped channel on the posts (or nail 1" x 2" pine strips) and slide the lattice downwards into position between the posts. Figure 5-5 shows a close-up of the lattice in the channel.

STEP ❻

Install the top rail with the attached channel over the lattice. Figure 5-6 shows the finished panel.

STEP ❼

To finish the job, add the finial of your choice to cover the post top and protect it from rotting.

PROJECT 6: MAKING A WINDOW BOX

Figure 6-1

I have found that the best way to make a wooden window box last for years is to use plastic window boxes as inserts. For this project, I bought two plastic window boxes and built the wooden casing to go around them. This method has several advantages. You can use the plastic window box to start your flowers under grow lights indoors or in the greenhouse, then set them into the wooden box when the weather warms up and the plants are almost in flower. At the other end of the season, it is easy to remove the plastic flowerbox, empty and clean it in preparation for next year. This method also allows you to install the wooden portion of the flowerbox in a permanent location where it can be screwed or bolted in place.

⚒ TOOLS

» Saw
» Screwdriver or hammer

OPTIONAL TOOLS

» Table saw
» Power screwdriver

↖ MATERIALS

» Two 8" x 1/2" x 30" boards for the front and back
» Two 8" x 1/2" x 9" boards for the ends
» One 30" x 9" x 1/2" board for the base, with holes drilled to let water out
» Screws or Nails: 1-1/4" galvanized or ceramic-coated #6 wood screws, or 2" finish nails

MATERIALS NOTE: I RECOMMEND USING DURABLE WOOD SUCH AS CEDAR, PAINTED PINE, WALNUT, OR TEAK TO STAND UP TO THE WEATHER.

Figure 6-2

🕐 TIME

Approximately 1 hour per window box

✋ METHOD

These directions explain the methods for creating both a free-standing and a wall-mounted window box, as shown in Figures 6-1 and 6-2.

STEP ❶

Cut the wood to size. If making the free-standing window box, both end pieces will be tapered as shown in Figure 6-1. Cut the two end pieces 8" at the top and 6" at the bottom and the two long sides to the dimensions show in the Materials section. For the wall-mounted box, the end pieces will have the mounting side edge vertical and the front edge sloped as shown in Figure 6-2. You can make the back side slightly taller (up to 10") to make mounting easier. Cut the long edges of the base piece to match the cut slope of the sides (ideally on a table saw). Drill six holes, three pairs of two, in the base piece for drainage. Figure 6-3 shows an exploded view and all the parts.

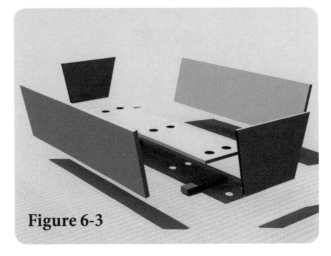

Figure 6-3

STEP ❷

Glue and screw or nail the sides and ends together to form an open box.

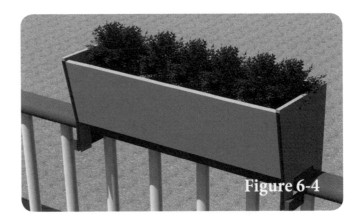

Figure 6-4

43

✋ METHOD

STEP ❸

Dry fit the base to make sure it fits. When you are satisfied with the fit, glue and screw or nail it into place.

STEP ❹

Install the window box in its final location.

Figure 6-5

⤻ OPTIONS

If you'd like to make a window box to sit on top of a deck rail, the end pieces should be brought below the rail with a notch cut out to allow the box to sit on the rail as shown in Figure 6-4.

Figure 6-5 shows cleats attached to the notch, which allow the box to sit on the rail without having to screw it directly to the rail. The cleat can be removed and the box can be lifted off the rail.

You can also make a series of boxes for many plants or one longer box up to about 4' long. (Any longer and you'll have to install a correctly sized brace to keep the long sides from bowing out in the middle.)

PROJECT 7: PICKET FENCE

Building a picket fence can be a long job, especially if you are starting from scratch. By building the fence in sections up to 8' long, the job can be reduced to a simple repetitive effort than can be finished in a few days. It takes about one to two hours to build an 8' section, depending on the amount of detail that you decide to incorporate into it and the shape of the top of each picket.

Here we show two fence options and several top details. The easiest method is to set up a table saw jig to cut each picket to the same length. If you decide to make

When I first moved into my house, my wife suggested that we get a picket fence to go around the garden. "The pickets will help to keep the deer out," she said. It was only after the 4' high fence was built that I found out that deer could leap over a 6' fence!

an 8' section with 1" x 2" pickets, spaced 4" apart, you will only need to cut 24 pickets per section. If you decide to space your pickets closer, say 2" apart, you will need 48 pickets per section.

Each picket is screwed to two 2" x 3" x 8' backing pieces, long enough to be lap-jointed or tenoned into a support post. It is easier to build using lap-joint cuts rather than mortise and tenon cuts.

⚒ TOOLS

» Rotary saw or chop saw to make pickets. A chop saw can be set at 45 degrees and each picket can be jigged to make cutting the tops fast and easy.

» Screwdriver, nail gun, or staple gun to fasten pickets to longitudinal supports

OPTIONAL TOOLS

» Hole digger for support posts

🕐 TIME

Up to 2 hours per 8' section of picket. But if you set up a jig, you can cut that to under an hour per section.

＼MATERIALS

FOR ONE 8' FENCE SECTION

» Two 3" x 3" wooden posts

» Two 2" x 3" x 8' boards for the longitudinal crosspieces

» Twenty-four 1" x 2" x 3' or 4' pickets (for 4" spacing; 48 pickets for 2" spacing)

» Caps or finials for the posts

» 1 1/4" galvanized or ceramic coated screws, four per picket, or 1 1/4" galvanized nails. I found that as the wood ages, nails tend to loosen in their holes and pickets fall off.

MATERIALS NOTE: BUY 1" X 3" PICKET WOOD TO SUIT YOUR FENCE HEIGHT, THEREBY REDUCING WASTE. FOR EXAMPLE, IF YOUR FENCE IS TO BE 3' TALL, BUY 12' LENGTHS AND CUT EACH INTO FOUR 3' PIECES. IF YOUR FENCE IS TO BE 4' TALL, BUY 8', 12', OR EVEN 16' LENGTHS AND CUT THEM INTO 4' PIECES..

YOU CAN USE 1" X 3" X 8' BOARDS FOR THE LONGITUDINAL CROSSPIECES, BUT THEY WILL EVENTUALLY SAG, MUCH MORE QUICKLY THAN 2" X 3" BOARDS.

METHOD

STEP ❶

Cut your pickets to size. You can make the top of your pickets any shape you like, and you may even want to make the top of the fence wavy for a different look. Figure 7-1 shows picket shapes and a wavy-topped fence.

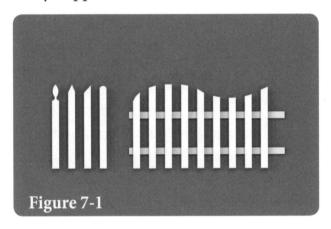

Figure 7-1

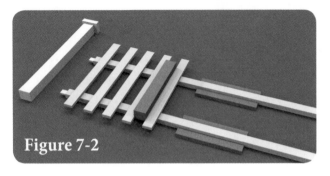

Figure 7-2

STEP ❷

When all the pickets have been cut, you'll want to make a jig to ensure that each 8' length of fence is identical. The jig can be set up on a single sheet of 1/2" or 3/4" x 8' plywood. Position two 1" x 3" blocks or cleats to hold the end of each longitudinal crosspiece in place. For a 3'-high fence, each fixture pair can be mounted so that the center of the cross-pieces are about 6" or 8" from the top and bottom putting the longitudinals 20" or 24" apart. For a 4' fence the longitudinal supports are 12" from the top and bottom putting them 24" apart. Screw or nail the cleats to the plywood base to make your jig. To space the pickets correctly, you'll also need a 2" or 4" wide spacer (equal to the length of your picket) Figure 7-2 shows how a jig is set up.

STEP ❸

With the cross-pieces set in place on your jig, it is time to start laying the pickets. Make sure the ends of the crosspieces are perfectly aligned, and lay your first picket 4" from the end (assuming that you are using 4" spacing between pickets). Then screw, staple, or nail it in place. Position your spacer as shown in Figure 7-3 and lay the second picket. Screw it into place. (For longevity, you might also want to add a little construction adhesive behind each picket. My experience suggests that the pickets are the first thing that falls off the fence as it ages. The only problem with using adhesive is that repairs can only be done by replacing entire sections of fence.) Keep laying pickets and fastening them in place until you reach the end of the rail section. Remove it and begin a new section. Once you get into the swing of things, you will find that you can build a fence section in 10 to 15 minutes.

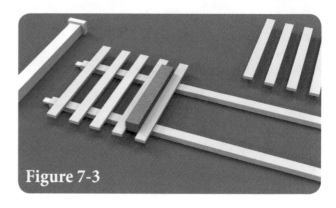

Figure 7-3

STEP ❹

Dig holes for your posts. If your soil is rocky like mine and you cannot get each post into the ground as far as needed, you will end up with posts at different heights (trim them after the fence is in place.). Thus you will not be able to cut lap joints or mortises until the post is firmly tamped into the ground. For this reason it is easier to make a lap joint in the back of the post after it has been set in the ground. Make your lap cut using a rotary saw set to the thickness of the 2" x 3" support board. When the lap has been cut out, screw the section into place overlapping the post by half to allow for the next section to be screwed to the post. Figure 7-4 shows a finished section of fence with square finials on the post tops.

Figure 7-4

⼁ OPTIONS

You can make the fence using dowels instead of pickets. Holes are drilled in the top and bottom supporting crosspieces through which the dowels are inserted. (Hint: Sandwich top and bottom cross-pieces, clamp them together, and drill both holes at once.) Secure each dowel with a nail or screw through the crosspiece (Put the screws in from the back where they will not be seen.) Figure 7-5 shows a fence using dowel pickets, while Figure 7-6 shows how the dowels are fitted through the longitudinal supports. Like the flat pickets, you can shape the top of a dowel picket any way you like. The top can be cut square, at an angle, or pointed. You will probably need access to a lathe to make the tops pointed.

Figure 7-5

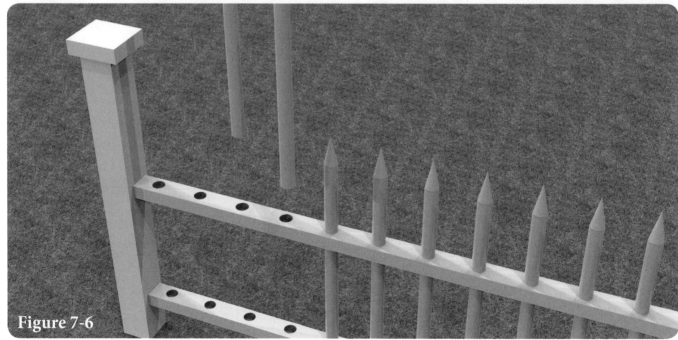

Figure 7-6

PROJECT 8: MAKING A LATHE TABLE

A simple but very strong table can be made from leftover scraps of wood from your picket fence project. Or you can make it from a more durable wood such as oak or cedar and use it on your deck or patio.

This table makes an attractive decorative piece for the garden, either on its own or with your prized potted plants or sculpture set on top. The unconventional design uses lath wood similar to picket, but set on edge with gaps to make an interesting tabletop and legs. If you like, you can make it out of a more durable wood such as oak or cedar and coat it with varnish to make it an attractive display in your garden. To create the tabletop with gaps, cut some laths into shorter sections and leave 2" to 3" gaps in the tabletop. Figure 8-1 shows how the tabletop is assembled.

TIME *With all the wood cut to length, assembly is limited by the curing time of the epoxy. Many products set up within an hour. If you think assembly will take longer, use a slow-curing epoxy to give yourself more time.*

⟍ MATERIALS

FOR ONE 4' X 3' TABLETOP WITH 15" LEGS

» Two or more 1" x 3" x 4' lath boards for both edges and one or two additional 1" x 3" x 4' boards to be positioned near the middle of the table (If you plan to curve the ends of the table, you will need to make the middle pieces 5' long instead of 4'.)

» Two 1" x 3" x 3' lath boards for the tabletop end caps

» Various lengths of 1" x 3" lath boards to fill out the tabletop. You can use short or long off-cuts from other projects. There are no set parameters for the length of each piece. (You might want to coat each piece with epoxy before you start. When the table is assembled it will be tedious to coat the ends of each piece of lath.)

» Four 1" x 3" x 15" lath boards for the table legs (Adjust the length if you wish to make your table higher. For example, if you wish to make your table 20" high use four lengths of 1" x 3" x 20" lath. To continue the tabletop theme in the legs, use eight same-sized lengths and add various lengths of 1" x 3" material to make four legs. Each leg would have two pieces of 1" x 3" lath on each side and the middle filled with short lengths of 1" x 3". The tops of the legs would slot into the tabletop.)

» Epoxy to glue the tabletop pieces together (Screws are likely to split the thin wood.)

» Varnish to protect the tabletop and prevent UV degradation of the epoxy

⟋ TOOLS

» Rotary saw or chop saw to make laths

» Screwdriver, nail gun, or staple gun to fasten laths in place

✋ METHOD

STEP ❶

Make a jig to cut all laths to approximately the same length.

STEP ❷

The tabletop is best assembled upside down to allow the legs to be more easily inserted. However, if you use epoxy to glue the lengths of wood together, any drips will glue your tabletop to the work surface. To avoid this, assemble the table top on a jig. Set a full sheet of plywood on your workbench and screw a length of 2" x 4" x 6' (or the length of your table) along one edge. Lay a sheet of construction polyethylene over the plywood to prevent the table top from being glued to the plywood.

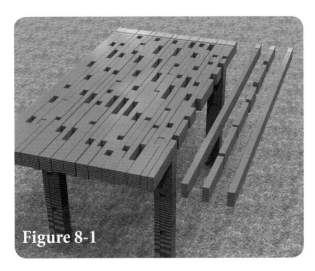

Figure 8-1

STEP ❸

If you wish to protect the table top from the elements, "paint" each piece of wood with epoxy or varnish before you start. Set the first strip of the table top against the 2"x 4". (The polythene will be over the 2" x 4" and under the strip to prevent the strips from being glued to the plywood.) Wear rubber gloves for this part. (I wear two pairs to allow for the top pair to be easily replaced.) Paint the entire inside length of the strip with epoxy.

STEP ❹

Take two short lengths of 1" x 3", say 6" long, and coat on side with epoxy on the sides. Set them at each end of the first strip. Fill the space with random lengths of 1"x 3" strips and clamp them to the first strip. Now take a longer strip of 1" x 3" strip, paint it with epoxy on one side and set it against the clamped pieces to start row three. Make sure it overlaps any gaps. Fill in row three, making sure you overlap any gaps. Clamp them in place.

STEP ❺

You might want to let the first three rows set up before starting on the fourth. I have found that if you clamp too many rows before the epoxy sets up, the table top may bow slightly.

STEP ❻

The fourth strip will begin with long pieces (up to 15") at each end and shorter pieces overlapping each of the pieces on the third strip.

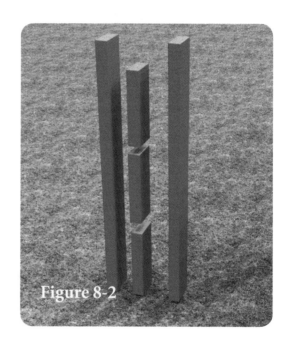

Figure 8-2

STEP ❼

Between the fourth and fifth strip is a good place to insert the table legs. These should be placed 6" from each end of the table. (If you are going to build each leg from two long strips with short pieces sandwiched in between, preassemble the legs on your work surface before starting work on the tabletop. Figure 8-2 shows an exploded view of one of these legs.) Figure 8-3 shows how the legs are inserted.

STEP ❽

Assemble each layer in turn until you have reached the desired width for your table. Remember to insert the other legs between the fourth and fifth strip from the other side of the table as you work toward the finish. Clamp the entire job into place and let dry for at least 24 hours. (Wrap your clamp ends with polyethylene to prevent them being glued to the tabletop.)

STEP ❾

When the tabletop is completely dry, lift it off the polyethylene sheet and discard the sheet. Sand the top and bottom to remove any epoxy or glue buildup. Apply two coats of polyurethane varnish. You now have an attractive table ready for display in your garden.

Figure 8-3

Fill these planter boxes with petunias, geraniums, or dianthus and a few lobelia and enjoy them all summer long.

What is the difference between a planter box and a window box? Mostly a question of size and placement. A window box is usually set on a window or other ledge or screwed to a wall beneath a window. A planter box is a larger ornamental box that usually sits on the ground. A filled planter box is heavy and can be an immovable barrier, so make sure that you have positioned your box properly before you fill it.

You can make any style of planter box, such as the square or tapered planters this project describes. These can be made larger or smaller, taller or longer, and they can be made of virtually any wood, although teak, cedar, and pine are the most popular. If you make your planter from pine, you may want to paint it to make it last longer than a few seasons. Also to make your planter last, you can put a potted plant inside the planter and fill the surrounding void with wood chips or mulch to hide the plant pot. Like the window box in Project 6, this extends the life of your planter by minimizing the amount of water that comes in contact with the wood when you water your plants. These planters are very heavy when filled, so you may want to make the plant dolly shown in Project 4 to move the plant and planter around.

MATERIALS

FOR THE SQUARE PLANTER

» One plywood piece for the base (The corners of the base will be notched out to fit around the corner posts.)

» Four 2" x 2" corner posts, with height to suit the pot size (To ensure that the posts stand above the plywood sides, you should add 4" to the pot height to calculate the post height. Thus, a one gallon pot, which usually stands 9" tall, will require 2" x 2" x 13" posts.)

» Four 2" x 2" top and four 2" x 2" bottom rails, with length to suit the pot size (These rails are mortised into the corner posts, thus 2" will need to be added to the length to accommodate a 1" deep tenon on each end of the rail.)

» Four marine-grade plywood pieces for the sides

MATERIALS NOTES:

USE A DURABLE WOOD SUCH AS CEDAR, PAINTED PINE, WALNUT, OR TEAK. TO MAKE THE TAPERED PLANTER, YOU MIGHT WANT TO USE A MARINE-GRADE PLYWOOD, WHICH WILL NOT DELAMINATE WHEN IT GETS WET. YOU WILL ALSO WANT TO INSTALL CLEATS ON THE BOTTOM TO RAISE THE PLANTER OFF THE GROUND.

BECAUSE PLASTIC POTS VARY SLIGHTLY IN SIZE WITH STYLE, MEASURE YOUR POT BEFORE MAKING A PLANTER. THE IDEAL IS TO MAKE YOUR PLANTER JUST SLIGHTLY LARGER THAN THE PLASTIC POT. USE THE TABLES BELOW TO DETERMINE THE SIZE OF MATERIALS BASED ON THE TYPE AND SIZE OF PLANTER YOU WISH TO BUILD.

⚒ TOOLS

- » Saw
- » Screwdriver or hammer
- » Framing square
- » Tape measure

OPTIONAL TOOLS

- » Table or rotary saw
- » Portable screwdriver

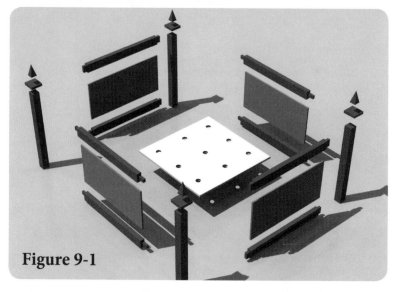

Figure 9-1

POT SIZE	SQUARE PLANTER BASE SIZE (PLYWOOD)	POT HEIGHT	CORNER POST SIZES	TOP AND BOTTOM RAILS	SIDES (PLYWOOD)
ONE GALLON	9" X 9"	9"	2" X 2" X 15"	2" X 2" X 9" (ADD 2" FOR TENONS)	9" X 7"
THREE GALLONS	11" X 11"	10"	2" X 2" X 16"	2" X 2" X 11" (ADD 2" FOR TENONS)	11" X 9"
FIVE GALLONS	12" X 12"	10"	2" X 2" X 16"	2" X 2" X 12" (ADD 2" FOR TENONS)	12" X 8" OR 9"
TEN GALLONS	15" X 16"	12"	2" X 2" X 18"	2" X 2" X 16" (ADD 2" FOR TENONS)	16" X 12" OR 14"

✋ METHOD

SQUARE PLANTER METHOD:

STEP ❶

Cut all material to the right size.

STEP ❷

Cut the mortise and tenon joints. (See "Making a mortise and tenon joint," page 61.) for instructions. Dry fit the parts and take them apart. Figure 9-1 shows an exploded view of the square planter box.

STEP ❸

Cut a 1/4" to 1/2" deep groove (dado) along one long edge of each rail to hold the sides in place. If you wish to make the planter really tight, you might want to cut dadoes in the uprights as well. If you do cut grooves, make sure that you increase the size of your plywood by the depth of all the grooves—top, bottom, and sides. So, a 1/4" dado on all four sides will increase the size of the plywood width and height by 1/2" each.

STEP ❹

Assemble a side. Take two posts, remembering to orient all the mortise joints correctly. See Figure 9-1. Apply glue to the mortise and tenon joints for the bottom rail and insert into the posts. Apply glue to the dadoes and insert the side panel, then glue and insert the top rail. Clamp everything tightly until the glue dries.

STEP ❺

Assemble the opposite side as in Step 4.

STEP ❻

Connect the two sides. Apply glue to the bottom rail tenons and insert into the mortises. Apply glue to the panel edges and insert into the dadoes. Glue and insert the top rails. After gluing, clamp the rails to ensure a good bond. Do not clamp so tightly that you squeeze all the glue out of the joint. Use a framing square to check that the sides are perfectly square. Pin each joint in place with a 1 1/2" finish nail hammered into place on the inside of the box.

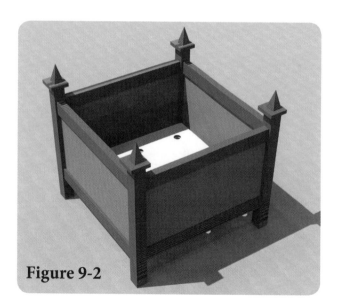

Figure 9-2

STEP ❼

Cut the bottom panel to fit by notching out the corners around the upright posts and resting it on the bottom rails. You will need to drill up to eight 1/2" diameter holes in the bottom panel (see Figure 9-2) to allow for drainage. You can leave the bottom panel loose to make it easy to clean your planter or you can screw it into place, using 1" #6 wood screws around the edges.

STEP ❽

Allow 24 hours for the glue to dry, put your planter where you like, then place your potted plant in the planter.

MAKING A MORTISE AND TENON JOINT

A mortise and tenon joint is a slot (mortise) into which is fitted a matched cut end (tenon), making a tight, clean join.

MORTISE: Locate the center of the top of the post on the side to receive the mortise cut. Measure two inches down from this center point, then 3/8" out to each side. Mark two straight parallel lines two inches down from these two points. Using a mortise chisel, cut a slot in the post 1" deep x 3/4" wide along these parallel lines. Repeat this procedure from the bottom of the post for the bottom rail. Repeat entire procedure for other three posts.

TENON: Mark two parallel lines on each end of a 2" x 2" cross bar 3/8" out from the centerline. Measure 1" along the length of the cross bar at each end. This will give you a 7/8" x 2" x 1" piece of scrap on the outside of each end of the cross bar. Using a tenon saw cut away that portion of each side. The tenon you have just created should fit perfectly in the mortise in the post. Repeat this for the other seven cross bars.

ⴑ OPTIONS

If you wish, you can screw wooden balls or finials to the tops of the posts for extra adornment. Instead of a plywood bottom, you can use wooden slats to allow easy drainage.

MATERIALS

FOR THE TAPERED PLANTER

» Four marine-grade plywood pieces for the sides. (The top width will be 1 or 2 inches wider than the base dimension. Thus, the one gallon pot tapered planter will require four pieces of plywood, each 9" at the bottom, 11" at the top, and 11" high. If you plan on using top and bottom rails like the square planter, you will have to adjust the size of the plywood to suit.)

» One plywood piece for the base (If you want to raise the planter on 1" x 1" cleats, the base should be cut 1/4" larger all round and the edges angled to suit the slope of the sides.)

» Four 1" x 1" boards, cut to the proper length to serve as cleats to fit the base (Miter cut the ends at 45 degrees to form flush corners.)

TAPERED PLANTER BASE (PLYWOOD)	BOTTOM OF SIDE (PLYWOOD)	TOP OF SIDE (PLYWOOD) FOR A GREATER SLOPE ON THE PLANTER INCREASE THIS DIMENSION BY 2"	HEIGHT (PLYWOOD)
9" X 9"	9"	11"	11"
11" X 11"	11"	13"	13"
12" X 12"	12"	14"	14" OR 16"
16" X 16"	16"	18"	16" OR 18"

METHOD

TAPERED PLANTER METHOD:

In many ways this planter is simpler to build than the square one, as there are no rails to shape and fit. The tapered edges of the planter are miter cut to ensure a strong joint, although you can put small 1" x 1" x 4" cleats along the inside of the glued joints to ensure they will not break apart when it is filled with soil or heavy pots.

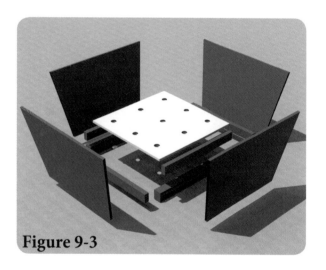

Figure 9-3

STEP ❶

Cut the sides and base to suit the size planter that you want to build. Miter cut the tapered edges of the planter at 45 degrees to ensure a strong, flush joint. I found it easiest to build this planter upside down by setting all four sides in place with the edges glued and clamping them together. Use a framing square to check that the planter corners are absolutely square. Figure 9-3 shows an exploded view of the tapered planter.

STEP ❷

After the glue has dried, remove your clamps and turn the planter over. Fasten small 1" x 1" x 4" cleats to the inside corners low enough that they will be covered with wood chips or dirt when the planter is filled.

STEP ❸

Glue and screw the bottom cleats to the bottom of each side. These cleats will support the baseboard.

STEP ❹

Drill up to six 1/2" diameter holes in the base board for drainage, as shown in Figure 9-4, and set it on the cleats that you have just installed. For a better fit, you might want to miter the sides of the baseboard to suit the slope of the planter sides.

STEP ❺

Allow 24 hours for the glue to dry, put your planter where you like, then place your potted plant in the planter. Figure 9-5 shows the finished planter.

Figure 9-5

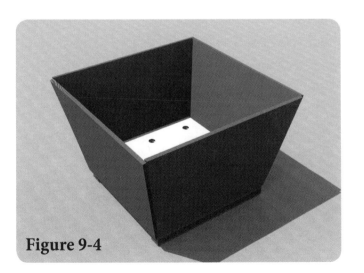

Figure 9-4

This potting table keeps all your potting supplies, tools, and spare pots in one place.

This is a slightly more ambitious project, but every garden shed or greenhouse will need a potting table. The doors on this table are designed to be locked to prevent small children from coming in contact with any pesticides that you might want to store. There is also enough space to store small bags of potting soil and other amendments.

The top has low side walls to help prevent potting soil from spilling over. There is also a handy large hole to one side of the table positioned over a shelf that holds a trash can to allow for easy disposal of scraps and any mess. I have also found that by cutting the hole of the right diameter, it can also serve to hold a plant pot while it is being filled with potting soil.

It's best to use marine grade plywood for the top and sides of the table, so that it can easily be hosed off, if necessary. If you wish, you can build the table from a fancier wood such as oak with oak-faced plywood if it is to be placed in a prominent location. The entire table is intended to be compact, easy to use, with good storage.

⏱ TIME

This project might take as long as two or three days to complete, not including glue-setting time.

MATERIALS

» Four 2" x 2" x 36" boards for legs

» Six 1" x 2" x 24" boards for side cleats

» Four 2" x 2" x 40" boards for front and back cleats

» Two 24" x 30" x 1/4" plywood for ends (If using angle brackets for the trash bucket shelf supports, make one of these pieces from 1/2" plywood)

» One 30" x 40" x 1/4" plywood piece for the back

» One 4 1/2" x 52" x 1/4" plywood strip for the back of the tabletop

» Two 4 1/2" x 30" x 1/4" plywood strips for the sides of the tabletop

» One 24" x 40" x 1/2" plywood for the base, or floor of the table (with corners notched for the support posts)

» One 12" x 40" x 1/2" plywood or 18" x 48" x 1/2" plywood for the cabinet shelf

» One 30" x 52" x 1/2" plywood for the top

» One 10" x 24" x 1/2" plywood for the trash bucket shelf

» Two 6" x 11" x 1/2" plywood for the shelf supports (or two angle brackets. If you use angle brackets, make the 24" x 30" end piece these are anchored to from 1/2" plywood.)

» Two 20" x 30" x 1/2" plywood for the doors

» Four 3" brass hinges for the doors

» One trash bucket (or make one from scrap plywood—use the smallest size tapered planter plan in Project 9.)

FASTENERS:

» Epoxy or any high quality exterior grade glue will do.

» Screws and Nails: 1-1/2" and 2" #8 brass or stainless steel wood screws to screw the supporting structure together, and 1" and 1-1/2" finish nails to nail the plywood to the structure

⚒ TOOLS

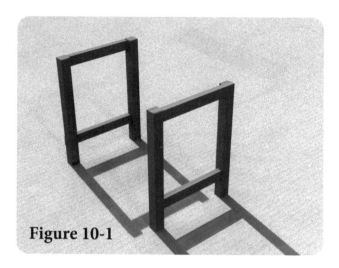

Figure 10-1

» Screwdriver or hammer
» Rotary or hand saw
» Large hole saw or hand keyhole saw
» Measuring tape

OPTIONAL TOOLS

» Table saw
» Router or dado saw

✋ METHOD

STEP ❷

Install the front and back cross bars into the end pieces using lap joints to form the frame of the table. Figure 10-2 shows the table at this stage. Install the shelf support cross bars.

STEP ❶

Make the end supports of the table first using the four legs and the six side cross bars. Each side cross bar is set into the post using a simple lap joint. The top cross bar is level with the leg top, the bottom cross bar is 6" up from the leg bottom, and the shelf cross bar is 13" inches up from the bottom cleat, putting the shelf 15" from the bottom. Figure 10-1 shows the assembled posts and cross bars.

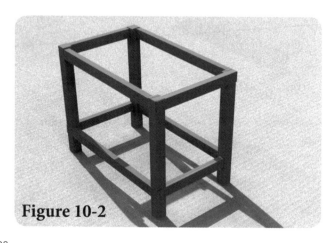

Figure 10-2

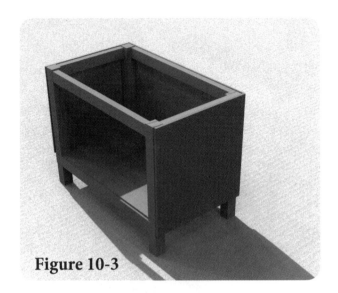

Figure 10-3

STEP ❹

Install the base, shelf, and tabletop using the 1/2" plywood pieces and 2" screws. (Figure 10-4 shows the end piece removed to show how the shelf is installed.) Install the tabletop with a 2" overhang at the left side and back and a 10" overhang over the right side above the trash can shelf. Figure 10-5 shows the table without the top at this stage.

STEP ❸

Cover the sides of the frame with 1/4" plywood as shown in Figure 10-3.

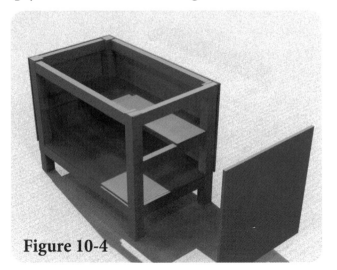

Figure 10-4

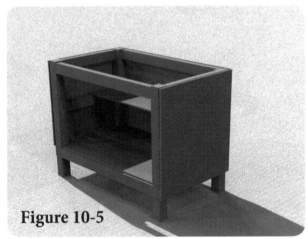

Figure 10-5

STEP ❺

Install the shelf support brackets. If you plan on using plywood as shelf supports, cut two 6" x 11" x 1/2" plywood pieces and trim a 4" triangle off the lower outer corner. The 6" high, 1/2" wide slot is best cut into the table end with a rotary saw before the table end is installed. Simply

Figure 10-6

mark it off two inches in from the outer edge with the top face of the shelf support directly against the shelf cross bar on the inside of the table. The actual height of the shelf will depend on the height of your trash can, so you should buy or make your can before installing this shelf.

When the plywood for the table end is installed the supports can be pushed

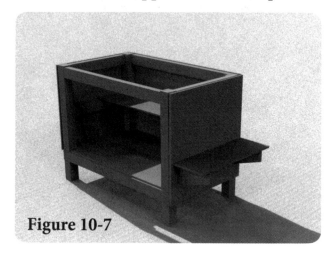

Figure 10-7

through the slots and screwed to the inside face of the table leg using 1 1/2" screws, as shown in Figure 10-6. Install the trash can shelf on the plywood cleats as shown in Figure 10-7.

(If using angle brackets, measure 6" or 8" up from the plywood, depending on the height of your trash can. Make sure both brackets are level and screwed into the table legs or shelf cross bar.)

STEP ❻

With the tabletop in place, measure a 5" or 6" diameter hole directly over the wastebasket. The trash can hole can be cut in several ways. The easiest, if you own a table saw is to put a 6" diameter hole cutting bit in the table saw and cut the hole before installing the tabletop on the project. If you do not own a table saw, do NOT try to use a 6" diameter hole cutting bit with a hand drill. Mark out a 6" diameter hole with a compass and drill a 1/2" hole inside the perimeter. Use a jigsaw to cut around the circle. (If you wish, you do not even have to make your hole a circle, you can make it square or oblong.)

If you wish you can put a piece of bungee cord around the wastebasket to hold it in place.

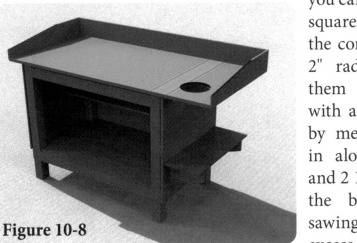

Figure 10-8

STEP ❼

Cut the 4 1/2" plywood tabletop borders as shown in Figure 10-8. Use a table saw set at 4 1/2" inches. Cut all three pieces needed at this setting. For the side pieces you can leave them square, round off the corner using a 2" radius or cut them as shown with a rotary saw, by measuring 10" in along the top and 2 1/2" up from the bottom and sawing away the excess.

Glue and screw the side and back strips to the edges of the tabletop, by drilling up through the tabletop from underneath and gluing and screwing the edge piece in place. If you are worried about splitting plywood, simply add a 1" x 1" trim strip under the tabletop and glue and screw the plywood to it using 3/4" wood screws or #4 finish nails.

STEP 8

Attach the doors. The hinges will be bolted to the doors, spaced 3" from the top and bottom of the door, and to the plywood sides. As the doors are only 1/2" plywood, you might want to add a 2" x 3" block to the inside of the door to which the hinges can be screwed. Attaching a block also on the outside of the plywood sides will lessen the chances of the door being pulled off should a child swing on it.

STEP 9

Paint or stain your potting table to suit your desired decor. If you did not make the table from marine grade plywood, it is recommended that you varnish the top to prevent water damage.

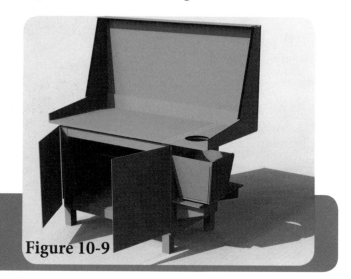

Figure 10-9

⑂ OPTIONS

You can also purchase a section of kitchen countertop if you want to make the potting table a little more fancy.

You might also want to put the table on casters to enable it to be moved around your greenhouse or potting area easily. Or you can add large wheels to one end and extended arms/handles under the countertop to enable it to be moved easily.

You can also add a backboard to the potting table as shown in Figure 10-9. If you use a peg board or similar material, tools can easily be hung on the backboard.

PROJECT 11: A PICNIC TABLE

Picnic tables can be made for the beach, dock, backyard, or anywhere that is likely to host a barbeque or fun time.

Picnic tables are easy to make and, for the cost of the wood, give you a useful outdoor table that will last for years. The only thing I would caution with these tables is that you should not sit four or five people on one side without a similar group to balance them on the other side!

I recommend using pressure-treated wood for the legs, which are in direct contact with the ground. The rest of the table can be made of regular, untreated wood.

TIME *4 to 5 hours*

⟀ TOOLS

- » Screwdriver or hammer
- » Rotary or hand saw
- » Large hole saw or hand keyhole saw
- » Measuring tape

OPTIONAL TOOLS

- » Table saw
- » Router or dado saw

⟍ MATERIALS

- » Nine 2" x 6" x 8' boards for tabletop and seats (Round off the outermost table top corners with a 3" radius saw.)
- » Two 2" x 4" x 27" cross braces to secure the tabletop
- » Four 2" x 6" x 36" boards for legs (You will need to cut angles at top and bottom.)
- » Two 2" x 6" x 60" boards for seat supports (Round off the bottom outer corners with a 3" radius saw.)

- » Two 2" x 4" x 24" boards for longitudinal braces
- » Four 3 1/2" x 3/8" bolts with washers and nuts to bolt seat supports to table legs
- » 2 1/2" #10 or #8 galvanized or ceramic-coated screws to assemble the table

✋ METHOD

STEP ❶

Assemble the top. The tabletop will be 30" wide (actually 27 1/2" wide because of dimensional lumber sizes) by 8' long. Lay out and align five 2" x 6" pieces of lumber side-by-side on a flat surface and screw the 27" long cross braces to them. Locate the cross braces exactly 9" from the each end of the underside and screw them in place, as shown in Figure 11-1. (The legs will also be screwed to the inside face of these cross braces.) If you screw through the underside of the cross braces to the table top, you will not have any screw heads showing on the table top.

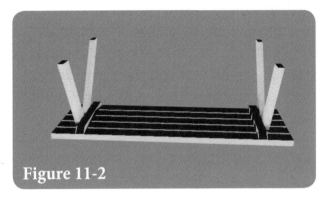
Figure 11-2

STEP ❷

Attach the legs. Position the legs so that the width across the top outside edges of the legs is 18" and the bottom outside edges is 56". Make sure they're centered. Figure 11-2 shows the table to this stage.

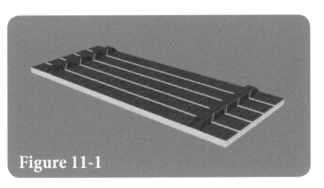
Figure 11-1

STEP ❸

Screw and bolt the seat supports to the legs with the top of the support exactly 14 1/2" from the bottom of the leg, as shown in Figure 11-3. This gives a seat height of 16". Use two screws to hold each seat support to the legs and then drill and bolt the seat supports to each leg using the four 3/8" bolts.

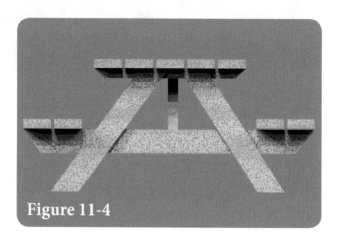

Figure 11-4

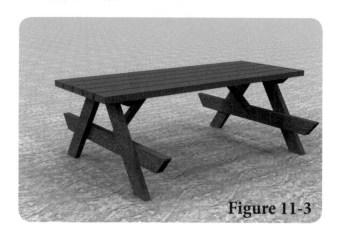

Figure 11-3

STEP ❹

Install the 2" x 4" longitudinal braces to increase the rigidity of the legs. These are 24" long with a 45-degree angle on each end. They are screwed to the underside of the table and the seat support. Figure 11-4 shows the center brace from the table end.

Figure 11-5

STEP ❻

That completes the basic construction of your picnic table. If you wish, you can sand and paint it, but most people leave the wood to turn silver. I would suggest that you roll wood preservative or sealer on the table top and seats to prevent them splintering after a year or three of use.

STEP ❺

Turn the table upright and screw the seats into place. Use two 2" x 6" x 8' seat pieces for each seat and position them at the outer ends of the seat supports. If you wish, you can round off the outer corners of the seats with a 3" radius. Figure 11-5 shows the finished table, and Figure 11-6 shows an exploded view.

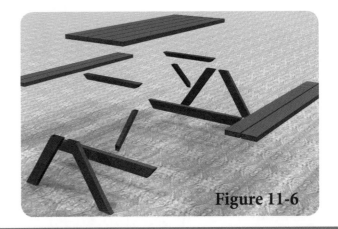

Figure 11-6

⤵ OPTIONS

You can build a mini picnic table for children as well. The table is also made of 2" x 4" lumber. In this case, the dimensions are: table width, 18"; length, 30"; height, 19" or 20"; seat height, 10"; length of seat support, 37"; tabletop cleat location, 8" from end of table.

Any home with small children needs a swing set. This one is easy to make and stays rigid as long as the posts are firmly embedded in the ground.

Because the posts are subjected to a lot of strain, take your time selecting them and buy posts with straight grain running as parallel to the edge as possible. There should also be as few knots as possible on the support posts or the cross bar.

This project includes instructions for building a simple swing set and a more involved set with monkey bars.

A swing set can be a fun item for children to have around the yard, especially when your children are young. Swing sets can be made well or they can be problematic. In order to keep this set in one position, the supports are dug into the ground. But swings get a lot of use and a smart homeowner will monitor the movement of the legs and ensure that they are firmly fastened down before kids play on them.

⚒ TOOLS

» Either a post-hole digger or a spade to dig the post holes
» Saw
» Chisel
» Drill with a bit sized for 1/2" bolts, and a bit for 3/8" rope
» Wrench for 1/2" bolts

OPTIONAL TOOLS

» 1" diameter bit for dowels
» Wrench for bolts for angle brackets

⟍ MATERIALS

For swing set

» Four 4" x 4" x 12' posts with straight grain
» Two 2" x 6" x 6' boards for cross braces
» One 4" x 4" x 4' post for top brace
» Bolts: Four 1/2" x 6" galvanized bolts with coach washers and nuts (two per bipod legs).

For swing set with monkey bars

» Add two more 4" x 4" x 12' posts
» Add a third 2" x 6" x 6' board
» One 4" x 4" x 10' top brace
» Two 2" x 6" x 8' boards for the sides of the monkey bar frame
» Two 2" x 6" x 2' boards for the ends of the monkey bar frame
» Two 4" x 4" x 9' posts
» Four 4" x 4" pieces of scrap lumber for support bracing
» Ten 1" x 24" dowels
» Two 3 1/2" x 3 1/2" angle brackets

» Eight 1/2" x 6" galvanized bolts with coach washers and nuts. (Cut off over-length bolts to ensure they cannot catch children's clothing.) Four or six (depending on the number of holes in the angle bracket) 1 1/2" x 3/8" bolts for each angle bracket.

⏱ TIME *1 to 2 days*

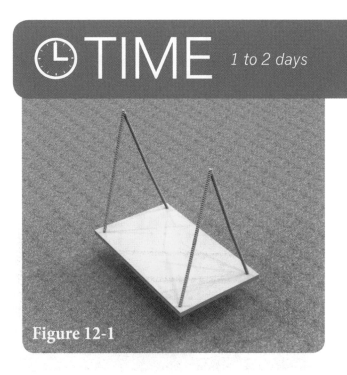

Figure 12-1

✋ METHOD

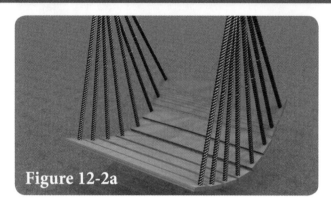
Figure 12-2a

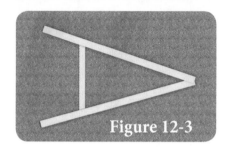
Figure 12-3

STEP ❶

The first step is to build your swing seat. This can be as simple as a 2" x 10" x 18" wooden plank as in Figure 12-1. (The narrower you make the seat, the more restrictive it will be. For example, a swing for an adult should be about 20" between the ropes. For a child, this distance can be as narrow as 14" or 16".)

If you plan on making the more complex swing as in Figure 12-2a, you will need to know how to splice rope in order to make a loop splice to fasten the seat ropes to the ring. If you do not know how to splice you can tie everything in knots, but it will look ungainly. The slats are held in place with a rope or tape stapled to the underside of the seat as shown in Figure 12-2b.

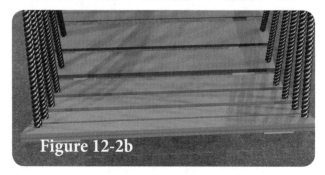
Figure 12-2b

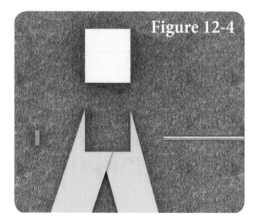
Figure 12-4

STEP ❷

Build the A-frames for the swing set. (You will need to make two support A-frames.) Lay out the support posts on a flat piece of ground. The bottom of the posts should be exactly 8' apart and the tops pushed close together as shown in Figure 12-3. Cut the support posts to fit them to the crossbar as shown in Figure 12-4. This will give you a swing support bar height of 9' 3" off the ground. When they have been cut, install the cross braces 48" up from the base of the posts. (The posts will be buried for two feet, so the cross braces will only be 24" off the ground.)

STEP ❸

Dig holes at the proper distances from each other. The two A-frames for the swing will be 4' apart. Bury your posts at least two feet in the ground. Tamp the soil around the posts down well. Check that your A-frames are straight. Now bolt the swing support bar to the top of the A-frames as shown in Figure 12-5. You might want to bolt a steel plate or a plywood gusset across the top of the A-frame to help ensure the wood will not split.

STEP ❹

Install the ring bolts for the swing into the swing support bar and set the swing in place. Adjust its height to suit the child who will be using the swing. Tamp the soil down around the posts again; add more soil and tamp down further if necessary to ensure stability.

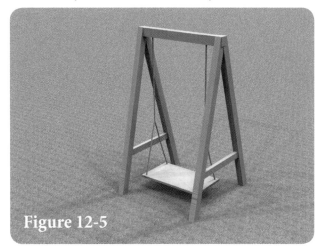

Figure 12-5

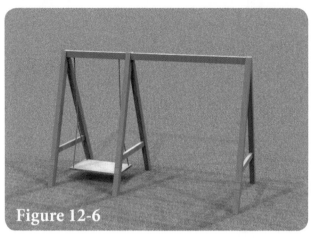

Figure 12-6

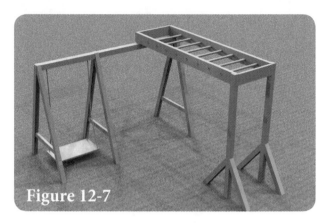

Figure 12-7

MONKEY BAR OPTION

STEP ❶

Follow the same procedure for the main swing set.

STEP ❷

Build a third A-frame.

STEP ❸

Set the third A-frame for the monkey bars 6' from that last swing A-frame. Install the 4" x 4" x 10' swing support bar across the top of the three A-frames, as shown in Figure 12-6.

STEP ❹

Install the ring bolts for the swing into the swing support bar and set the swing in place. Adjust its height to suit the child who will be using the swing. Tamp the soil down around the posts again; add more soil and tamp down further if necessary to ensure stability.

STEP ❺

Build the monkey bar box. First sandwich the two 2" x 6" x 8' side boards together and drill ten 1" holes evenly spaced along the boards. Then build a rectangular box as shown in Figure 12-9. Insert the dowels through the holes and glue them in place.

STEP ❻

Measure 8 feet out from the top brace and dig two holes, spaced 24 feet apart for the monkey bar support posts. Set the two 4" x 4" x 9' posts in place, tamping the soil around the posts well. Install support braces with 3/8" bolts.

STEP ❼

Hoist the monkey bar box onto the supports. Attach box to the top bar of the swing set with 3 1/2" x 3 1/2" angle brackets with 3/8" bolts to the support posts. Figure 12-7 shows the swing with monkey bars, and Figure 12-8 shows the monkey bars set alone.

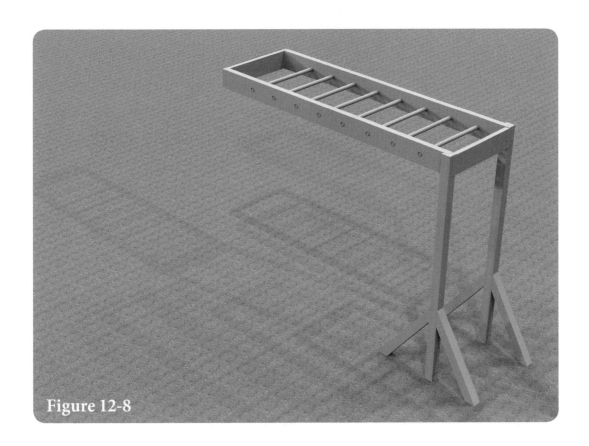

Figure 12-8

This simple birdhouse can be painted in many ways to differentiate it from its neighbors.

Making a birdhouse is an ideal beginner's woodworking project. This project can be built by virtually anyone using just a saw, a drill, a screwdriver, and a few screws. All you need to do is transfer the measurements in the materials list to a piece of pine board and saw along the lines. The six pieces of pine board required cost only a few dollars. So experiment and improve your carpentry skills.

Differently sized birdhouses and entrance holes will attract different bird species. This project design will work for birds such as chickadees, titmice, and wrens. A little additional research will help you tailor your birdhouse to whatever species you'd like to attract.

 TIME *1 to 2 hours per birdhouse, depending on how ornate you want to make them*

✎ MATERIALS

» One 1" x 6" x 48" plank of pine lumber, from which will be cut:

- Two side pieces, each 4" wide x 7 3/4" tall at the back—one piece 5 1/2" and another 6 3/4" at the front
- One 5 1/2" x 8" back piece (Cut the top on a bevel to suit the slope of the roof.)
- One 4" x 5" front piece (Again, cut the top edge on a bevel to suit the slope of the roof.)
- One 4" x 4" base piece

- One 4 1/2" x 9" top piece (If you want a 1" overhang on each side, make this piece 6" wide instead of 4 1/2".)

» Paint or stain as needed

» Hardware mesh for squirrel protection

FASTENERS:

» #10 brass or stainless steel screws at least 1 1/2" long (I prefer to use Phillips head screws.)

⚒ TOOLS

» Rotary saw, table saw, or handsaw to cut out the parts

» Screwdriver

» Paint brush or roller

» Drill with a 1 1/4" bit

» Wood glue

✋ METHOD

STEP ❶

The basic birdhouse shown here consists of six pieces—base, front, back, two sides, and roof. They can all be cut from a single 1" x 6" x 48" plank of pine lumber, as shown in Figure 13-1 and described in the Materials section. (Note that what is called 1" x 6" lumber actually measures 3/4" x 5 1/2".) The slightly shorter sides allow for a 1/4" gap for air ventilation. Figure 13-2 shows how the air vent is positioned.

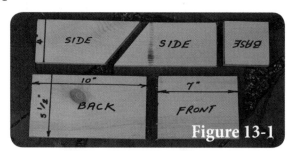

Figure 13-1

STEP ❷

Position and drill the 1 1/4" entrance hole in the front panel.

STEP ❸

Screw the sides to the front piece. If you have not beveled the top of the front and back pieces to suit the slope of the roof, temporarily screw the sides to the front and mark the bevel. Do the same with the back piece and then cut the bevels. Glue and screw the sides to the front and back pieces. Set the birdhouse on the base and glue and screw them together. Figure 13-3 shows an exploded view of the birdhouse.

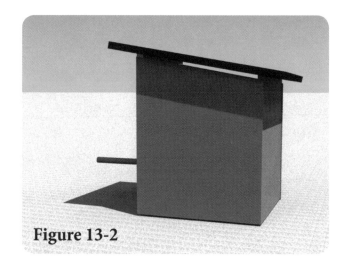

Figure 13-2

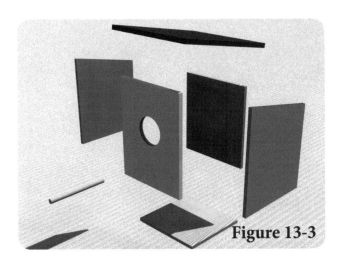

Figure 13-3

STEP ❺

Screw the top in place. Your birdhouse is now ready for use. You can mount it by screwing a cleat across the back or by screwing through the back into the post, fence, or wall where you plan to mount it. It is not recommended to screw a birdhouse to a tree. Hanging it from a limb with a hanger is best.

STEP ❹

The next decision is how the birdhouse is to be opened for cleaning. Making the top removable is easy to do but means that you must remove the birdhouse from its support in order to invert it for cleaning. Another way to open the birdhouse is to hinge the base piece downwards (as shown in Figure 13-4) so that you can simply scrape out old nesting residues. Attach a hinge to the outside of the back and the base and put a clasp at the front. If you do this, you will need to bevel the front face of the bottom plate to allow it to hinge up into the bird box.

Figure 13-4

⚡ OPTIONS

✳ UPGRADING THE BIRDHOUSE ✳

If you want to paint your birdhouse, now is the time to do so. If you leave it unpainted, the wood will eventually weather to a light gray and merge into the background. Brush painting, spray painting, or using a roller are your three options for applying color. If you are particularly artistic, you can also add decorative elements of any kind that you wish by painting

them on with a brush. There is no limit to the ways that this simple birdhouse can be upgraded. With a fertile imagination (and some help from your children), this project can be fun for the whole family. You might want to make your birdhouse into a Tiki bar, a thatched-roof Tudor house, or a shingled New England cottage, for example.

PROJECT 14:
ORNAMENTAL WHEELBARROW

Imagine having this wheelbarrow parked near your gate and filled with multicolored petunias or lobelia. It would lift your spirits when you drive home from a long day at work. Or you can put it on your deck and grow vegetables.

This wheelbarrow is not difficult to make, but it does require a little attention to detail. Like the planters and window boxes, the wheelbarrow can be made of pine, waterproof plywood, or a more ornamental wood such as cedar or teak. While it is much easier to go to a hardware store and buy a wheel or salvage one from an old wheelbarrow, I offer here a method for crafting your own wheel out of wood.

⚒ TOOLS

» Rotary saw or hand saw
» Plane or rasp
» Sandpaper
» Screwdriver or hammer
» Waterproof glue
» Paint and brushes (if desired)

OPTIONAL TOOLS

» A drill press for drilling the wheel hub

🕐 TIME *1 to 2 days*

↖ MATERIALS

- » Two 2" x 2" x 5' oak or ash boards for the handles. Round off the last 6" of the length for handles.
- » Two 1/2" x 4" x 3" scrap plywood pieces to hold wheel end of handles together
- » Two 1/2" x 2" x 2" scrap plywood pieces to hold the wheel axle in place
- » Two wedge-shaped wood pieces— measuring 2" x 3" at thick end tapering to 2" x 1/4" at narrow end, 20" long—as braces for the sides of the wheelbarrow box
- » One 1/2" x 20" x 20" waterproof plywood piece for the base
- » One 1/2" waterproof plywood piece for the wheel end of the cart, measuring 20" at the bottom, 24" at the top, and 14" high
- » One 1/2" waterproof plywood piece for the handle end of the barrow, measuring 20" at the bottom, 24" at the top, and 7" high

- » Two 1/2" waterproof plywood pieces for the sides, 20" long, 7" high at the back, and 14" high at the front
- » Two 2" x 2" x 16" boards, with ends cut as shown in Intro picture to support the front of the wheelbarrow.
- » Two 2" x 2" x 14" boards as legs for the wheelbarrow
- » Two 2" x 2" x 14" boards, with ends cut at 45 degree angles, as braces for the legs.
- » 1/2" waterproof or marine grade plywood for the wheel, which can be between 6 and 10 inches in diameter with 8" being the most common. Figure 14-1 shows it as four-spoked, but you can make it with six or eight spokes, if desired.
- » Four 1 1/2" x 8" x 12" boards for the spoked wheel
- » One 1 1/2" x 30" dowel
- » Waterproof glue and screws for the wheel as indicated in the text

✋ METHOD

Building the wheelbarrow begins with the wheel. If you have a wheel from an old wheelbarrow, by all means use it. If you don't want to spend time making a wheel, simply buy one. Most hardware stores offer some form of wheel.

However, if you want the added challenge of making your own wheel, there are two methods of making one, outlined below. The first is to cut out four or five pieces of 1/2" waterproof or marine grade plywood. The second is a spoked wheel with four separate quarter-circle pieces cut from a 2" x 8" board.

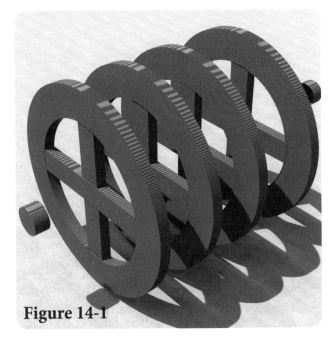

Figure 14-1

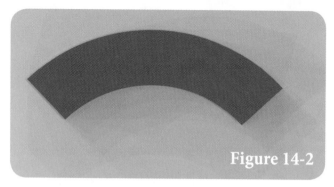

Figure 14-2

✳ PLYWOOD WHEEL ✳

STEP ❶

Scribe four 9" diameter circles on your 1/2" thick plywood. Mark out the number of spokes that you need. Four spokes are set at 90 degrees to each other, five spokes are set at 72 degrees apart, and six spokes are 60 degrees apart. For now, make each spoke about 1 1/2" wide. It will be made smaller later.

STEP ❷

Glue and clamp the four pieces together with the spokes lined up as shown in Figure 14-1. Add two small 1/2" plywood bosses, or blocks, on either side to bring the total width of the wheel to 3".

STEP ❸

When the glue is dry, unclamp the wheel and use a rasp to "round off" the spokes. How much you round them is up to you. Some owners may just sand down the sides of the spokes and leave them square. If you wish to hide the plywood edges you can cover the cut edges of the spokes with a 2"-wide strip of edge banding varnish or paint the entire wheel to protect it from rot and delamination.

STEP ❹

Drill through the center of the wheel to insert the axle. The axle can be made of 1/2" or 3/4" metal rod.

✺ SPOKED WHEEL ✺

STEP ❶

The outside arc of the this wheel is made in four parts. Cut each section from 2" x 8" lumber with the grain running along the axis of the curve as shown in Figure 14-2. (The curved portion is shown in a different color to the waste portion of the wood.)

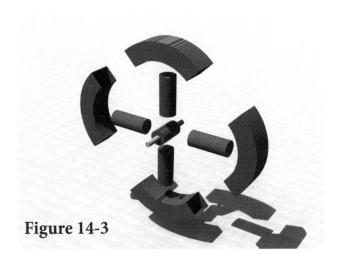

Figure 14-3

STEP ❷

Cut the 1 1/2" x 30" wood dowel into four 4" lengths for the spokes and one 3" length for the central hub. Cut the spokes slightly oversize, because you will want to sand both ends—to conform with the arc of the wheel and the curve of the hub dowel.

STEP ❸

Using a bench drill press, drill through the long axis of the center hub. This is the trickiest part of the entire operation. The dowel being used for the central hub will need to be set perfectly vertical in the drill press and care taken not to split the dowel when drilling.

STEP ❹

Glue and screw the spokes to the arc of the wheel. To fasten the spokes tightly, countersink and bung 3" #10 screws through the wheel rim. Then glue the hub into place. Figure 14-3 shows an exploded view of the wheel.

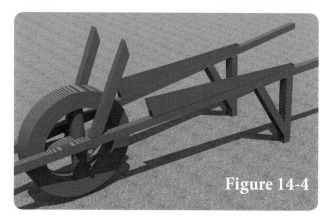

Figure 14-4

✳ WHEELBARROW ✳

This wheelbarrow is slightly larger than 24" x 24" at the top, and 20" x 20 at the bottom, with a taller 14" front than the 7" back .

STEP ❶

Make the handle/leg assembly.

Mark on the handles where the wheel axle will go. The axle of a 9" wheel will be 12" from the end of the arms. Glue and screw the wedge-shaped braces to the handles 16" from the front (wheel) end of the handles, the wider side toward the front, as shown in Figure 14-4.

Set the legs and the leg braces in place as shown in Figure 14-4. Fasten in place

with two 1/4" x 4" bolts drilled at an angle through the leg and the handle.

These parts will be set up as in Figure 14-5 to take the remainder of the barrow.

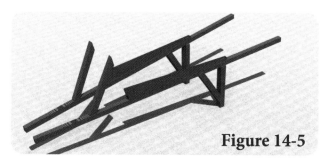

Figure 14-5

STEP ❷

Adjust your handle end width. Standard arm width at the handle end should be 21" to 22" apart. This spacing can be adjusted for the size of the person using the wheelbarrow. Then attach 1/2" x 4" x 3" scrap plywood pieces to the top and bottom of the front ends of the handles to hold them in place 4" apart. Use four or six 1 1/2" #8 wood screws on top and bottom to screw plywood to handles. Also attach two 2" x 2" pieces of scrap plywood under each handle to hold the wheel axle in place as shown in Figure 14-8.

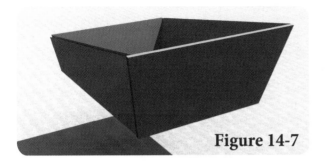

Figure 14-7

STEP ❸

Build the box separately as shown in Figure 14-7. The plywood should be glued and screwed together. If you plan in using the barrow for heavy duty work, install triangular cleats on the inside of each corner to help strengthen the box. Screw through the front panel into the supports using four 2" #8 wood screws.

STEP ❹

Bolt the box to the handles. Drill through the bottom about 4" to 6" from the front and back and bolt the box to the wedge portion of the handles using 3/8" bolts with washers. Use two 6" or 7" x 1/2" bolts at front and two 3" x 1/2" bolts at the back to hold the base to the handles. The bolts go through each handle, each wedge, and the plywood base.

STEP ❺

Attach the 2" x 2" x 16" wheelbarrow front supports. Position the support in place and mark the angle of the support on the side of the handle, so you can drill a 1/4" hole at this angle through the handle and into the support to receive the 1/4" x 4" fastening bolt.

STEP ❻

Install the wheel. Figure 14-8 shows the finished wheelbarrow.

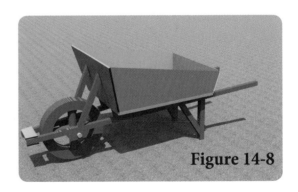

Figure 14-8

↱ OPTIONS

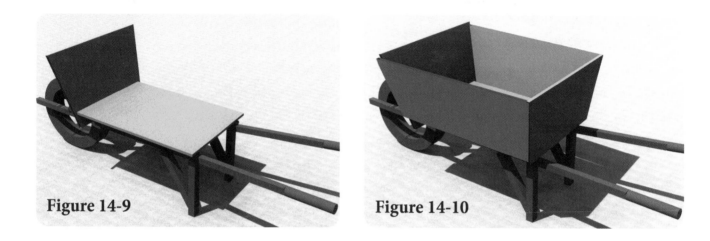

Figure 14-9

Figure 14-10

You can also make the wheelbarrow without sides as shown in Figure 14-9. This wheelbarrow is ideal for toting 3'- or 4'-long logs, large plant pots, or other gear that is too large for the conventional wheelbarrow. You can also make the barrow much deeper for loading lightweight materials as shown in Figure 14-10.

PROJECT 15: A MOVEABLE RAMP

You have probably never given it much thought, but lifting a barbecue grill, getting a wheelbarrow onto a deck, or raising a kid's toy over the threshold can get to be quite a chore, especially if you have to do it ten or twelve times one after another. Here's a simple 3' x 4' ramp to eliminate the difficulty of lifting heavy wheeled objects to clear a threshold. I also describe the extra steps and sizes necessary for a 4'-wide ramp. As an additional option, I show how to build a wheelchair ramp with very specific dimensions to make it easy to get a wheelchair up steps.

A ramp can save your back. A simple ramp leading up to your deck makes it easy to push a grill or cart onto your deck or patio. A ramp can also make a deck or front door accessible for a wheelchair-bound person.

⏱ TIME

About 2 hours

↗ TOOLS

» Hand saw or rotary saw
» Screwdriver
» 5" x 3/8" bolts for handrails

97

MATERIALS

» One 2" x 8" x 4' or 2" x 10" x 4' board depending on finished ramp height

» Eight 2" x 6" x 3' boards for the floor of the ramp

FASTENERS:

» Forty-eight 3" galvanized or ceramic-coated exterior screws (Ceramic are best, as galvanized screws may rust over time.)

✋ METHOD

STEP ❶

Cut the 2" x 8" x 4' (or 2" x 10" x 4') on the diagonal to get two triangular-shaped pieces, with 1/4" height at one end and 7 3/4" (or 9 3/4") at the other end. (For a 4'-wide or wider ramp, install a third triangular-shaped piece along the centerline of the ramp to ensure it is strong enough to support a heavy load.) Set the two triangular pieces of wood exactly 2' 9" apart for a 3'-wide ramp. (For a 4'-wide ramp, set the pieces 3' 9" apart with the third piece on the centerline as shown in the exploded view in Figure 15-1.)

STEP ❷

Screw the first 2" x 6" floorboard in place at the high end, using three screws per contact point. Then working down the ramp, screw the rest of the floor boards in place. You should end up with maybe half an inch of triangular piece left over. Simply trim it off.

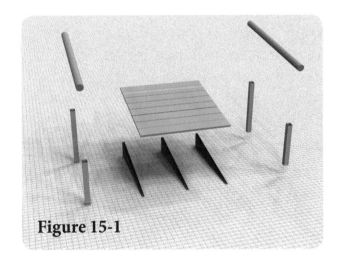

Figure 15-1

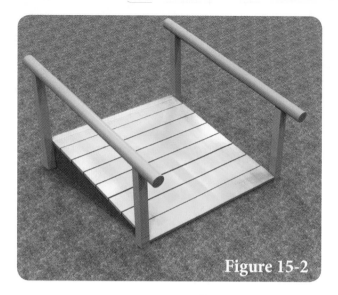

Figure 15-2

STEP ❸

Paint your ramp, if desired. Because it is sloped, you might want to put some form of non-skid material in the paint. I recommend Interlux's Interdeck paint, a marine product intended to prevent slipping on boats. You can also purchase Intergrip, a compound with tiny plastic spheres, and sprinkle it onto the first coat of wet paint. Then roll a second layer of paint over it. Regular sand will eventually work its way out of the paint. Also, you will have created sandpaper and, if you slip, we all know what that does to knees and elbows.

STEP ❹

Add handrails if the ramp is to be permanent. Handrails are simple to add and need to be between 32" and 36" high depending on the height of the person using the ramp. Bolt four 3" x 3" posts to the support boards at the four corners of

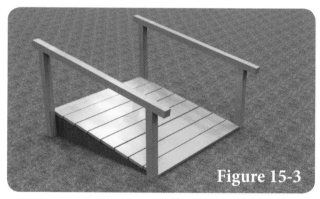

Figure 15-3

the ramp (you will have to cut away edges of the ramp floor). Then measure your desired rail height on the post and cut the top at the same angle as the ramp. Then screw a handrail or 2" diameter dowel to the top of the support post as shown in Figure 15-2. Figure 15-3 shows square handrails that can be rounded off slightly with a plane.

⤴ OPTIONS

✳ A HANDICAPPED-ACCESSIBLE RAMP ✳

A wheelchair ramp is a more complex project. (Check local building codes prior to construction for any specific requirements for residential homes.) To begin with, it is a permanent structure, so the support posts will need to be sunk into the ground, and the base support pieces will need to be notched into the posts 2" above the ground so they won't rot. Also, a handrail is a necessity. The grade should not be more than one inch over every twelve inches (a 1/12 grade). Also, in terms of the length, there should be a flat resting place every 12 to 15 feet. Each turn should have a flat portion to allow the wheelchair occupant to turn the chair before embarking on the next sloping portion. Handrails are not required but recommended for ramps longer than 6 feet. This project describes the construction of a simple 3' wide by 12' long straight ramp leading to a flat platform.

MATERIALS

FOR A 12-FOOT RAMP

» Three 2" x 10" x 12' boards for the base supports
» Twenty-four 2" x 6" x 3' boards for the floor of the ramp
» Six 3" x 3" x 5' pressure-treated posts (to allow for a 32" handrail height and the sinking of the posts 2' in the ground)
» Two 12' lengths of 2" (minimum) handrail

FASTENERS:

» 216 3" galvanized or ceramic-coated exterior screws
» Twelve 7" x 3/8" or 1/2" galvanized bolts with coach washers to bolt the posts to the base.

TIME *6 to 8 hours*

METHOD

Figure 15-4

STEP ❶

As above, cut the 2" x 10" x 12' board in two equal pieces along the diagonal to use for the base supports. (Most wheelchair ramps are a minimum of 36" wide, but if you are building a wider ramp, use additional supports.) Figure 15-4 shows a profile view of the ramp with posts and rails.

STEP ❷

Set your 3" x 3" support posts approximately 2' in the ground (below the frost line) and evenly spaced along the 12' length. Cut a lap joint into the support posts 2" above ground to allow the 2"x10" base supports to land on solid wood. Figure 15-5 shows an exploded view of the ramp.

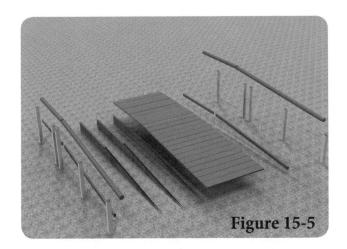

Figure 15-5

Figure 15-6

STEP ❸

As in the movable ramp project, screw the floor boards to the supports to form your ramp. Again, paint the ramp with a non-slip paint to make it easy to roll up and down on.

STEP ❹

Add handrails. For a person in a wheelchair handrails between 34" and 36" high are best. Figure 15-6 shows the finished ramp with handrails and also a flat platform at the high end of the ramp.

A few years ago, I was given five wood-framed storm windows, each 30" wide, and decided that they would make a great cold frame for my garden. As the growing beds were already 4' wide (see Project 1) and the windows were 5' long, the cold frame's back height of 3' was simple to calculate (3-4-5 triangle). I built two triangular ends and a rear section and screwed the three parts together easily, after which the storm windows were simply set in place.

A cold frame can extend your growing period by two to three weeks at each end of the season. Cold frames can be made from old storm windows, spare panes of glass, or other recycled materials.

⚒ TOOLS

» Handsaw or rotary saw
» Screwdriver or hammer
» Tape measure

⟍ MATERIALS

» Two 4" x 4" x 4' pressure-treated posts for the back corners

FOR THE ENDS

» Two 2" x 4" x 3' boards

» Two 2" x 4" x 28" boards

» Two 2" x 4" x 22" boards (Tops will be trimmed to suit the slope of the triangle.)

» One 2" x 4" x 4' board for the base

» One 2" x 4" x 5' board for the hypotenuse

» Scrap barn board or siding to cover the ends, or one 1/2" x 3' x 4' marine-grade plywood sheet, cut in half along the diagonal

FOR THE BACK

» Two 2" x 4" x 12' boards for top and bottom rails

» Six to ten 2" x 4" x 3' boards for the supports for the top and bottom rails. (Spacing the supports 24" apart requires six supports, and spacing them 16" apart requires ten support posts.)

» Scrap barn board or siding to cover the sides, or one 1/2" x 3' x 12' marine-grade plywood sheet

» Five 30" x 5' wood-framed storm windows

FASTENERS:

» Either 16P nails or 3" galvanized or ceramic-coated exterior screws for the main framing

» 1 1/2" 6P or 8P galvanized exterior nails for installing the plywood.

TIME

I built my cold frame in about 8 hours but your actual time will depend on the type of windows or glazing that you use.

✋ METHOD

STEP ❶

Sink the 4' posts 1' deep into the ground at the two back corners of the bed.

STEP ❷

Build the rear frame. Lay the top and bottom rails out on a flat surface and screw or nail the support posts in place at 16" or 24" intervals along the rails.

STEP ❸

Build the end triangle frames. Make sure the tallest post is the same height as the rear section (nominally 3') with the triangular section tapering to nothing at the front. Space the supports and cut them to suit the end angle before nailing or screwing them in place.

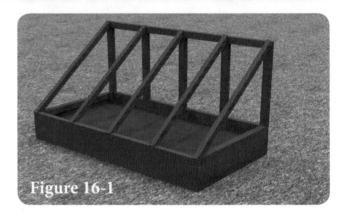

Figure 16-1

STEP ❹

Erect the ends and rear sections and nail or screw into place. The frame will now look like Figure 16-1. (This frame has four windows instead of the five that I built my frame with.)

Tip: Adjust the height and width of your cold frame to suit any storm windows. The only criterion is to have enough height at the front of the bed to allow vegetables to grow to their normal height.

STEP ❺

Clad the frame with siding. Size your siding to extend below the side of the frame in order to cover the air gap between the sections and the raised bed. Figure 16-2 shows progress.

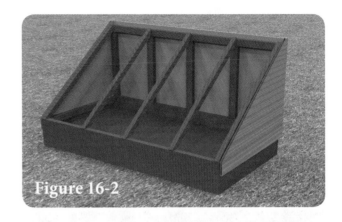

Figure 16-2

Figure 16-3

STEP 6

Set the windows in place. They do not need to be hinged, but you can install two 3" hinges at the top of each window to ensure the windows stay in place. A simple stick pushed into the ground in front of the frame will serve to keep the frame open as shown in the introductory picture.

Figure 16-4

We all want a garden shed. It serves as a place to keep almost everything that won't fit into the garage, except for the family car! This project describes the construction of a simple 8' x 12' shed that is large enough to house the lawn mower, rototiller, and all the other garden tools, including the barbecue grill and outdoor chairs and table in winter. You can also make a larger shed and turn it into a small workshop, a man cave, or any other type of hideout. The choice is yours.

The basic principles are the same for a shed of almost any size, although you may have to increase lumber sizes if you make the shed larger. This shed has one door with a small window in the front and a larger window in the back, but you can customize it to your liking, by adding more windows and doors, a dormer to increase the size of the shed, or other additional features.

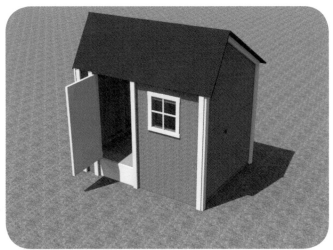

A garden shed may seem like a daunting job for a novice builder, but break it down to its components, and it becomes a manageable task.

⏱ TIME

About 4 days, but embellishments and extras can extend it to a week

⚒ TOOLS

- » Rotary saw or hand saw
- » Builder's square
- » Pencil
- » Screwdriver
- » Electric drill with #40 bit for wood screws and Phillips head bit
- » Hammer

- » Ruler or measuring tape
- » Putty knife
- » Sandpaper (various grades)
- » Paint (undercoat and topcoat in the desired color)
- » Wood putty

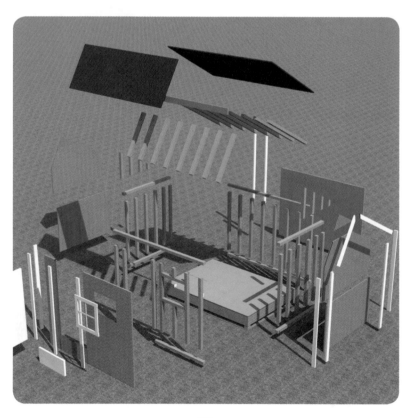

MATERIALS

FOUNDATION

LUMBER:

» Two 6" x 6" x 8' (or 8" x 8" x 8') pressure-treated posts

» Two 6" x 6" x 12" posts

» Four 4" x 4" x 3' lumber with ends cut to a point. These pieces will be hammered or dug into the ground at the corners to anchor the shed firmly.

FOUNDATION FASTENERS:

» Either 16P nails or 3" galvanized or ceramic-coated exterior screws for screwing the corner posts to the foundation.

» 6" or 10" TimberLOK screws for the lap joints

FLOOR FRAMING

LUMBER:

» Nine 2" x 8" x 8' joists spaced 16" center to center.

» Two 2" x 8" x 12' joists for the sides.

» Three sheets of 1/2" plywood or underlay to cover joists.

REAR WALL LUMBER:

» Three 2" x 4" x 12' boards for sill plate and header plates

» Ten 2" x 4" x 8' boards for studs (Double the two end studs to allow for inner walls if desired.)

REAR WALL FASTENERS:

» If you recess the base into the support posts, use 3" galvanized or ceramic-coated exterior screws to hold the majority of the structural components together. To nail plywood to the framework use 1 1/2" #6 or #8 galvanized nails. Corner trim will require 2" #4 or #6 galvanized finish nails punched below the wood surface and puttied over.

＼ MATERIALS

FRONT WALL WITH DOOR AND WINDOW:

» Three 2" x 4" x 12' boards for sill plate and header plates

» Twelve 2" x 4" x 8' boards for studs (Double the two end studs to allow for inner walls, if desired. Make cripple studs for window.)

» One 23 1/4" by 23 1/4" sheet of glass for the window

» One door to fit the 37" x 79" opening (either pre-framed or not)

FRONT WALL FASTENERS:

» Either 16P nails or 3" galvanized or ceramic-coated exterior screws for the main framing

END WALLS:

» Six 2" x 4" x 8' boards for sill plate and header plates (three for each wall)

» Sixteen 2" x 4" x 8' studs (eight for each wall)

» Ten 2" x 4" x 8' studs for gable end (five for each end; studs cut to suit slope of roof.)

END WALL FASTENERS:

» Either 16P nails or 3" galvanized or ceramic-coated exterior screws for the main framing

ROOF

LUMBER:

» One 2" x 6" x 10' or 2" x 6" x 12" board for ridge pole

» Eight 2" x 6" x 8' boards for rafters

FASTENERS:

» Either 16P nails or 3" galvanized or ceramic-coated exterior screws for the main framing.

METHOD

Figure 17-1a

STEP ❶

Mark out the boundaries of the foundation. Before starting work, mark out the shed's location and measure the diagonals carefully to ensure that your shed base is perfectly square.

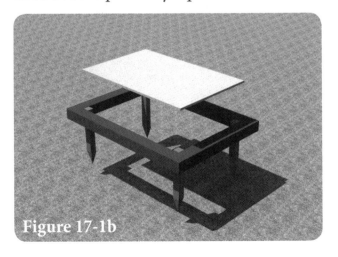

Figure 17-1b

STEP ❷

Build the foundation. Lay the 6" x 6" pressure-treated lumber on the ground (or dug slightly into the ground) around the edges of the marked foundation (after cutting lap joints on each corner of the foundation). Hammer the four 4" x 4" x 3' pressure-treated posts with the sharpened ends into the ground inside each corner to serve as anchors for the shed. Use 8" long screws to screw the 4" x 4" posts to the foundation boards. Figure 17-1a shows the foundation finished, while Figure 17-1b shows the component parts. The middle is filled with gravel on top of a sheet of heavy cardboard or polyethylene.

(A second method of building the foundation involves simply hammering the 4" x 4" posts into the ground and fastening the shed floor framing directly to the 4" x 4" posts. The downside of this approach is that this leaves the shed floating over the ground and may provide a hiding place for rodents and small animals. It also makes it difficult to insulate the underside of the shed of you plan on doing so.)

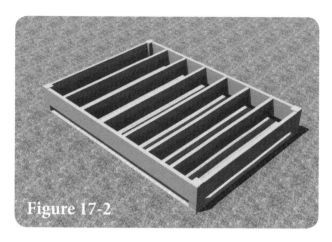

Figure 17-2

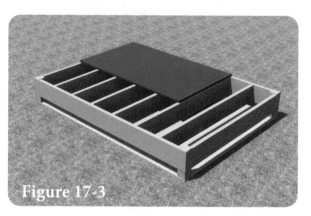

Figure 17-3

STEP ❸

Build the floor framing. My experience is that if you plan on insulating the floor, you should build the floor framing upside down, and screw or nail 3/8" or 1/2" pressure-treated plywood to the bottom of the floor. Make sure to notch out 4" x 4" holes at each corner for the corner posts. After installing the bottom plywood, turn the floor over and set it into place over the foundation. Hammer the corner posts into place and trim the tops level with the top of the base. Screw the base from the outside into the corner posts to firmly anchor your shed. Insulation can be placed in the base before it is covered with 1/2" pressure treated plywood.

Figure 17-3 shows the plywood going into place. It will take three sheets of 1/2" plywood to cover the floor. Note how the plywood joints are staggered, shown by different colors, in Figure 17-4.

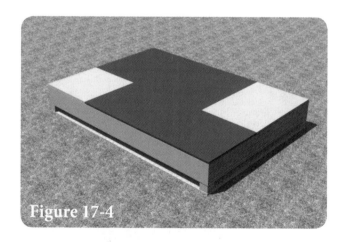

Figure 17-4

STEP ❹

Build the front and back walls. Lay out the materials and check the diagonals before nailing everything together.

For the back wall, space the 2" x 4" x 8' studs 16" apart and nailing them to the top and bottom 2" x 4" x 12' sill and header plates. If you plan on installing any kind of interior wall covering, you will need to add a second stud in the inside corner to allow for the covering to be fastened to the new stud.

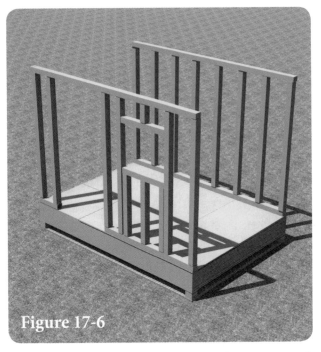

Figure 17-6

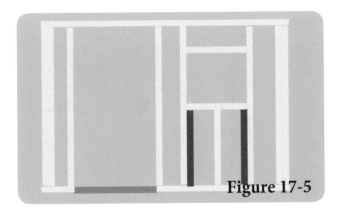

Figure 17-5

The front wall has a 3' wide door and a 24" x 24" window. The door is framed up leaving a 37" x 79" rough opening. (If you have the door in a frame, it can be set in place without leaving a rough opening.) The front wall is shown in Figure 17-5. Note the placement of cripple studs (shown in brown) to ensure the windows have enough support. The sill plate at the bottom of the door (shown shaded) will be cut away when the wall has been erected. When the walls have been built, they are erected as shown in Figure 17-6. (We have left out diagonal bracing for clarity.)

STEP 5

Build the end walls. These are framed using 2" x 4" x 8' studs and 2" x 4" x 8' top and bottom plates. You will need to cut the top and bottom plates to 7' 9" to allow them to fit inside the front and back walls. Figure 17-7 shows the framing so far. At this stage an additional 2" x 4" header plate is nailed around the top of each wall making sure that it overlaps at the corners to tie everything together.

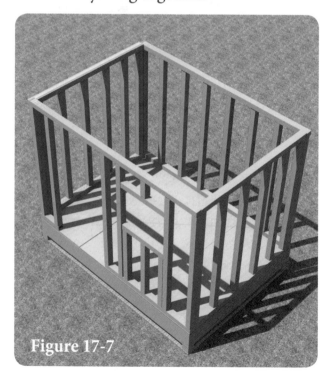

Figure 17-7

STEP 6

Install the gable ends. On the shed shown here, the ridge sits forward of the roof center to cut down on the amount of runoff water that falls down the front of the shed. (If you wish you can easily put the ridge in the middle of the shed roof or move it completely to the front.) The gable ends are two feet tall at the peak and are laid out as shown in Figure 17-8. Frame them up using off cuts of 2" x 4" studs. When complete position them on top of the end walls and screw or nail into place.

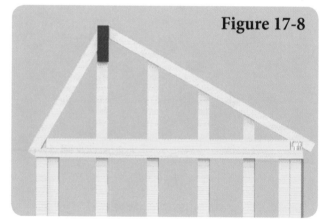

Figure 17-8

STEP ❼

Build the roof framing. Position the ridge pole and screw or nail it into place (shown dark brown in Figure 17-8.) The 2" x 8" x 12' ridge pole should drop into place in the slots in the end walls. With the ridge pole in place, the rafters can be cut and set up. Each rafter will have a "bird's mouth" notch in the bottom where it is fitted over the sidewalls and a sloped cut at the top where it rests against the ridge pole. When the rafters are cut, they are screwed or nailed into place at 16" on center, on both the sidewalls (by toenailing), and at the ridge. Figure 17-9 shows the bird's mouth feature, and Figure 17-10 shows the roof framed up.

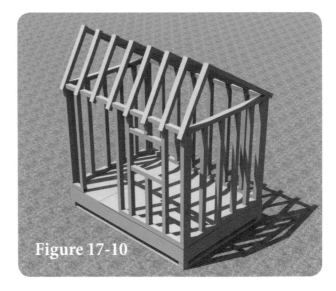

Figure 17-10

Figure 17-9

STEP ❽

Install the siding and roof covering. This shed uses barnboard panels nailed into place, as shown in Figures 17-11 and 17-12, but you can use any type of plywood siding and wrap the shed with Tyvek before installing wooden shingles or other form of covering. The roof is covered with tarpaper and regular roof shingles, as shown in Figure 17-13. One or two bundles of shingles will suffice.

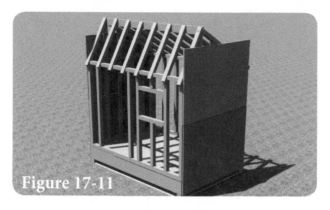

Figure 17-11

STEP ⑨

Install the door and window. First, trim the sill to the edge of the studs that will hold the door, as shown in Figure 17-5. Then hang the door with the appropriate number of hinges, or if you have a door already installed in a frame, simply attach the door frame to the studs.

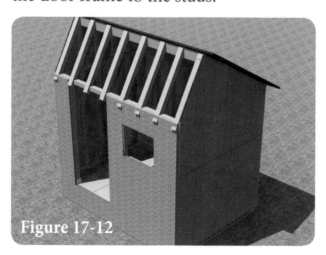

Figure 17-12

The window is made from a single 23 1/4" by 23 1/4" pane of glass (and thus cannot be opened). Frame the glass. With the 1" x 4" (actually 3/4" x 3 1/2") window framing, the entire window assembly will have a 24" x 24" exterior dimension. The framing should be painted before installing, or you can use one of the modern plastic trim materials to cut down on long term painting. Figure 17-14 shows the finished shed.

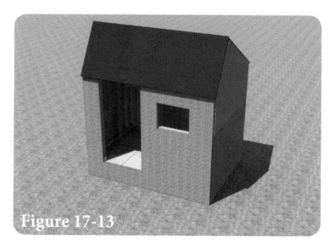

Figure 17-13

⌁ OPTIONS

Build the ramp in Project 15 to make it easy to take wheeled implements into the shed.

As mentioned in the text, the options for this shed are many. It can be made to virtually any size. It can be insulated in the floor and interior, and sheetrock or other covering can be applied to the interior walls. More windows or doors can be fitted. The roofline can easily be changed. The changes are only limited by your imagination.

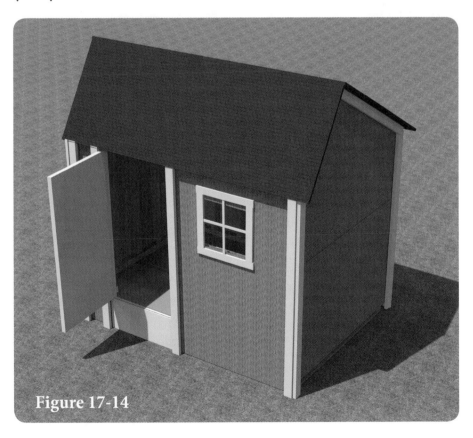

Figure 17-14

PROJECT 18: CELEBRATIONS

PROJECT 18A:
JULY 4TH FLAGPOLE

Your woodcraft skills can be put to good use livening up the holidays throughout the year. This section gives three ideas for three different holidays: Fourth of July, Halloween, and Christmas.

Making a flagpole uses the same technology a boatbuilder uses to make a wooden mast. The actual construction is not a huge project, but it does require a sharp plane and a willingness to sand and smooth the pole to get an evenly smooth surface. Depending on its length and where you'll be locating it, you can use one piece of wood for your flagpole or build it from several pieces. Single lengths of wood up to about 20' long usually have to be special ordered from most wood shops. (Sometimes a pole made of a single length of wood will warp, giving you a bent flagpole.) Poles longer than this will have to be made from glued sections.

This exercise describes the construction of an 18' pole from four pieces of 3" x 3" square wood, resulting in a 6" x 6" base. By orienting the grain in opposite directions, the tendency of a single length of wood to warp is removed. The pole is shaped by a process called chamfering, where the four 90-degree edges are planed down until the pole is rounded.

I also describe how to build a tabernacle, a device designed to hold the base of the pole while allowing it to be raised and lowered by one person. The tabernacle consists of two wooden "cheeks" spaced just wide enough to hold the pole. The cheek pieces are held together with a wood block at the bottom. A pin inserted through the cheeks and the pole holds the pole vertically in place. When it is to be lowered, the pin is removed and the pole is lowered down. The tabernacle should be secured by two metal plates concreted into place in the ground. (Alternatively, you can bolt the flagpole to the two steel plates for a permanently erected flagpole.) If you plan on leaving the flag up all night, you can also wire in lights for illumination.

⚲ TOOLS

» Measuring tape
» Clamps (enough to place one every 6" to 9" along the length of the pole)
» Wood planer (either hand or power planer)
» Electric drill
» Shovel
» Paintbrush

🕐 TIME

This project might take two or three weekends depending on how fast you plane wood.

↖ MATERIALS

POLE:

» Four 3" x 3" x 18' straight-grained pine boards for the pole (Mahogany can be used for short ornamental poles.)
The length of the pole determines the thickness of the pieces:

- Up to 6' long pole made of four 1" x 1" boards.
- Up to 12' long made of four 2" x 2" boards
- Up to 24' long made of four 3" x 3" boards.

» One or two cleats to tie the rope to (Ex.: Shaefer Marine Nylon 4" open base cleats # 70-94)

» Paint or varnish

TOP CAP:

» Ronstan nylon sheave #PNP98JR, with 12mm diameter (about 1/2") center pin, and 10mm (approx 3/8") or smaller rope

OR

» Ronstan Orbit block number RF35151, with 8 mm (3/8") or smaller rope

TABERNACLE:

» Three 2" x 4" x 12' boards for sill plate and header plates

» Ten 2" x 4" x 8' boards for studs (Double the two end studs to allow for inner walls if desired.)

REAR WALL FASTENERS:

» Metal plates 1/4" x 4" wide, depth to suit the depth of concrete, but I would suggest at least 12" and up to 24"

» One bag Quikrete

» One 3" x 6" x 6" wood block

» Two 2" x 6" x 3' boards

» Pin or bolt 10" x 1/2" diameter

» Waterproof glue (I prefer to use epoxy)

✋ METHOD

Figure 18a-1

STEP ❶

Glue your boards together. Figure 18a-1 shows the pole in four pieces. Start by gluing together two pieces of wood with the grain in opposite directions. Repeat this with the other two pieces. Then glue these two pieces together to get a pole made of four sections. Clean up any glue drips before they dry. Check for straightness before clamping everything tightly together. Figure 18a-2 shows the pieces before clamping. (A longer pole would require that the joints be staggered to give the pole longitudinal strength.)

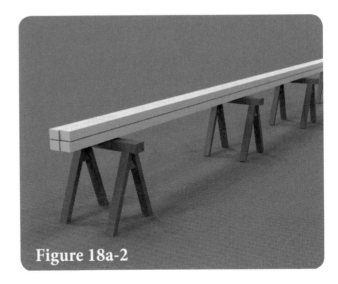

Figure 18a-2

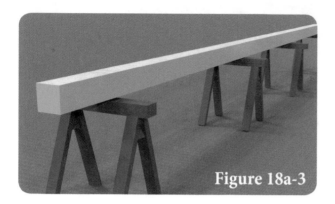

Figure 18a-3

STEP ❷

With the pole clamped together and the glue dry, check your pole for squareness and for straightness. If you are happy with it clean off any glue drips and mark out the first chamfer. Figure 18a-3 shows the pole glued, cleaned, and ready to be tapered. On this pole, we will keep the lower 3' square to allow it to fit into the tabernacle, thus our first chamfer will begin at the 3' mark. As the pole is to be tapered along its length it will be 6" diameter at the 3' mark and 3" diameter at the top. At the top, inscribe a circle 3" diameter and mark 45-degree chamfers as illustrated in Figure 18a-4. Note the chamfer lines are about 1/8" outside the top circle (black circle) to allow for adjustment when the pole is finish planed.

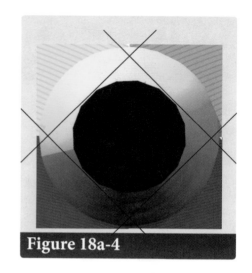

Figure 18a-4

STEP ❸

Plane off the first corner from top to bottom as shown in Figure 18a-5. Plane off the other three sides and you will have a result that looks like Figure 18a-6. Notice the top of the pole will gradually become square, but at 45 degrees to the bottom.

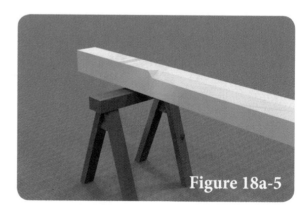

Figure 18a-5

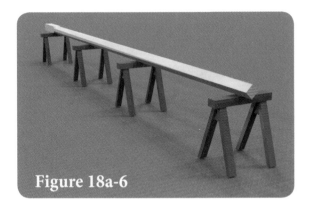

Figure 18a-6

STEP 4

Mark the top of your pole with the next set of chamfers as you did in Figure 18a-4. When these corners are planed down, the top of the pole will have eight sides.

STEP 5

Mark the next set of chamfers and plane the corners away to get sixteen sides at the top, as shown in Figure 18a-7.

STEP 6

Begin planing off each corner to make your pole round. You will find that you can do most of the rounding at this point by eyeball and then use 100-grit sand paper to make the pole completely round, as shown in figure 18a-8.

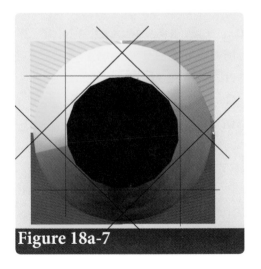

Figure 18a-7

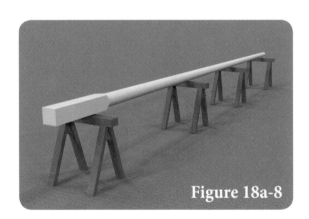

Figure 18a-8

STEP **7**

Make the top cap. Cut a piece of 2" x 8" x 8' and mark a 7" radius on the block. Trim corners at 45 degrees to make an octagon. Now trim the corners to give a sixteen-sided block. If you wish you can trim the corners again or sand the block into a circle.

When the block is circular, use either a router or sander to put a 3/4" radius on the top and bottom edges. This will give you a block that looks somewhat like a frisbee. To cut the holes for your pulleys you will need to make two 3/8" (or what width your pulley is) slots on each side of the block, with centers 5" apart. (Your flagpole top should be 4" diameter.) Cut the slots by drilling and chiseling then through the wood cap.

At the center of each slot you will need to drill from the side of the block through the center of the slot to fit the pulley pin. Insert your pulleys and set the pin in place. Use a wooden block or a strip of metal to cover the pin to prevent it falling out.

If you decide to insert a single pulley in the top of your pole, simply mark a slot 3/8" x 3" or the width and diameter of your pulley.) Drill through the top of the pole and chisel out the excess. Insert the pulley and drill from the side to set a pin through the center of the pulley. Again cover the pin head to prevent it falling out.

Figure 18a-10

If you prefer not to cut a slot in your flagpole use a Ronstan Orbit block number RF35151 (as shown in Figure 18a-10) screwed to each side of the pole top. To screw the block in place take a screwdriver and suitably sized woodscrews. Place the Ronstan block on the wood and insert wood screws in the holes in the pulley block. Using a screwdriver turn it clockwise to insert the screws into the wood. These use 8 mm (3/8") or smaller rope halyards.

STEP 8

At the bottom of the pole, install one or two small cleats, such as Shaefer Marine Nylon 4" open base cleats # 70-94. These should be placed just above the chamfer.

STEP 9

Cut the metal plates to shape and position over the hole in the ground in which you are about to pour concrete. I suggest that you make up a jig to hold the plates 10" apart and to the most suitable depth. Check that the tabernacle that you have just made will fit between the metal plates. Pour concrete around them and allow the concrete to set up before aligning the pole pins and screwing the tabernacle to the concrete plates. Glue and screw the 3" x 6" x 6" wood block into place at the base of and between the two upright 2" x 6" x 3' boards. Once the cement is dry, set this unit between the steel plates and drill holes to install bolts through the plates and the wood, as shown in Figure 18a-9. Drill a hole to fit your pin through the cheeks and the flagpole. To make the unit

Figure 18a-9

even more secure, the metal plates can be higher and the lower pin that holds the flagpole in place can be pushed through both the steel plates and the cheeks.

STEP 10

Paint and varnish your flagpole as desired. Set your pole upright and hoist your flag just in time for the Fourth of July.

Figure 18b-1

PROJECT 18B: HALLOWEEN TOMBSTONES

Make this graveyard part of your Halloween scene so that kids have to pass through it to get their candy. Adults will get a laugh from the humorous inscriptions carved into the tombstones.

These tombstones can easily be made from 1/2" or 3/4" plywood scraps, 1" wood scraps, or 1" rigid foam insulation. The "stones" shown here were made by my son and his college friends to decorate their dorm for Halloween. Adding a plastic skull or three, a ghost, a few candles, and even a smoke machine would give you a perfect eerie display.

⚒ TOOLS

- » Saw
- » Sharp chisels (for wood) or X-Acto knife (for Styrofoam)
- » Sandpaper, paint, and brushes for decorating the tombstones

＼MATERIALS

- » Any plywood scraps, 1"-thick wood scraps, or 1"-thick rigid foam insulation panels

⏱ TIME

Each panel will take about 1 hour to shape, although plywood will take a little longer. Carving the inscription might take an additional 1 to 5 hours, plus 2 to 3 hours to paint the tombstone. Painting the inscription will take less time.

✋ METHOD

STEP ❶

Check a few tombstones in your local area or online to get an idea of shapes and sizes. Dream up a few quotes such as:

HERE LIE THE BONES OF ARTHUR JONES,

ON HALLOWEEN NIGHT YOU CAN HEAR HIS MOANS

TIM TEDDER FELL INTO A SHREDDER

MAY HE REST IN PIECES

HARRY BROWN

FELL IN A WHISKY VAT AND DROWNED . . .

HAPPY

No doubt, you can think of a ton more to complete your graveyard.

STEP ❷

Cut out the tombstone shapes and paint them to look like old stones. Remember to add details like lichens and cracks. Either carve the epitaph into the wood or Styrofoam or paint it on.

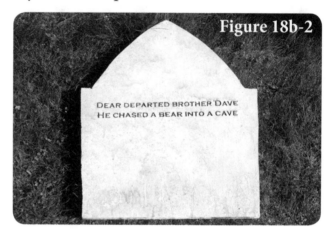

Figure 18b-2

DEAR DEPARTED BROTHER DAVE
HE CHASED A BEAR INTO A CAVE

STEP ❸

To set up your graveyard place the stones in a row where people have to walk past them, put a lit candle or low wattage light (to allow people to read the inscription), and wait for the laughs.

PROJECT 18C:
CHRISTMAS SLEIGH

This sleigh can be a fun and attractive addition to your Christmas display. You can make the sides from 3/8" plywood to keep it fairly light, but if you expect children to be playing in the sleigh, you should use 1/2" plywood for the sides and add a few additional braces to ensure that it will not collapse.

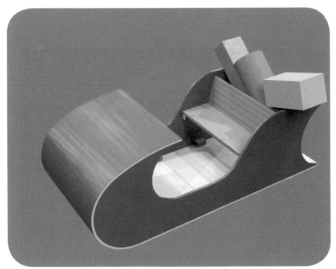

Snow falls gently on Santa's sleigh as it sits on the lawn. With a few lights and a little ingenuity, this project can light up your Christmas and bring good cheer to your neighbors. (Well, maybe!!)

↗ TOOLS

» Jigsaw or saber saw
» Rotary or table saw
» Sandpaper or power sander
» Screwdriver
» Electric drill
» Glue

MATERIALS

» Two 3/8" x 30" x 72" waterproof plywood boards for the sides

» Two 1/4" x 30" x 60" waterproof plywood boards for the curved front

» One 1/2" x 30" x 48" waterproof plywood board for the bottom

» One 3/8" x 6" x 30" waterproof plywood board to cover the join between the bottom and front

» Five 1/2" x 16" x 30" waterproof plywood boards or 1" x 16" x 30" boards for the foot rest, seats, and seat backs

» Twenty to thirty 2" x 3" x 4" scrap boards for cleats along sides (size can vary depending upon what you have on hand)

» Six 2" x 2" x 14" boards for cleats under seats and behind seat backs

FASTENERS:

» 2" #8 wood screws (preferably in brass or bronze to ensure they will not rust)

TIME

Eight to 10 hours to make the sleigh. Painting and detailing can add another 10 to 20 hours.

✋ METHOD

STEP ❶

To cut the side boards, first lay both boards flat on the ground and fasten them together. Using a compass to draw circles, draw a 30" diameter circle for the front of the sleigh (circle 1). A similar circle should be drawn for the back of the sleigh (circle 2), as in Figure 18c-1. A second 30" diameter circle (circle 3) should be drawn overlapping the aft-most circle by about 3". The two smaller 24" diameter circles (4 and 5) should be set 12 inches above the base line.

Now, join the two smaller circles at a horizontal tangent across the bottom and draw a fair curve up to circle 3.

Using a saber or jig saw, cut around the leading edge of circle 1, around the front of circle 4, across the bottom of circles 4 and 5, and up around circle 3. Cutting around circle 2 will give you the curved trailing edge for the sleigh.

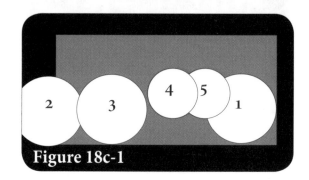

Figure 18c-1

STEP ❷

Cut out the sides of the sleigh, using a saber saw or jigsaw. Sand and trim the edges until you have removed any burrs and saw marks. The sides can be painted at this time. Figure 18c-2 shows the shape of the cut sides.

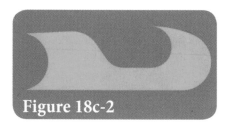

Figure 18c-2

132

STEP ❸

Cut 20 to 30 cleats to fasten to the sides. These cleats will be set along the sides to hold the curved front in place and secure the floor to the sides. Glue and screw the cleats along the edge of the sides, spaced about every 4 or 5 inches.

STEP ❹

Attach the bottom to the sides. It is best to work with the sleigh upside down at this stage. Set the bottom on the side pieces and glue and screw into the cleats. (Do not glue the sides to the bottom if you are going to break the sleigh down for storage.) Installing the rear seat and seatback at this point will help brace the sleigh (see steps 7 and 8), or you can temporarily brace the sides so that they do not collapse.

STEP ❺

Install the curved front pieces. You may find it easier to bend the 1/4" plywood front when it is wet, but try it dry first. If it shows signs of cracking, wet it down or use thinner plywood. First apply glue to the cleats. Then carefully bend the plywood around the front of the sleigh and screw it to the cleats.

STEP ❻

Let the first sheet dry and coat it with a waterproof glue. Take the second 1/4" plywood sheet and bend it over the first, gluing it into place. Driving a few screws into extra cleats will help fasten the second layer of plywood down tightly. Leave until the glue has dried. Remove any additional screws and fill the holes with nail-hole filler.

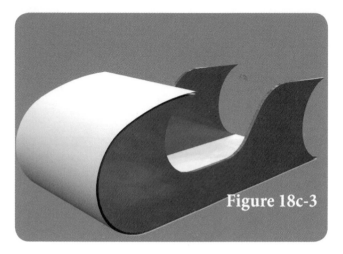

Figure 18c-3

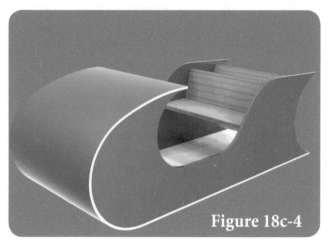

Figure 18c-4

STEP 7

Put the 6"-wide strip of plywood over the joint between the curved portion and the flat bottom on the inside of the sleigh. Glue and screw it into place to be sure that the joint will hold, making sure the screws are set into cleats. Turn the sleigh back upright. It should now look like Figure 18c-3.

STEP 8

Install the cleats for the footrest, seats, and seatbacks. Position the seat cleats so that they are comfortable for children, about 15 to 16" off the sleigh floor. Position the footrest cleats at a comfortable angle for resting your feet while seated. Position the seatback cleats by measuring a few inches from the back of the sleigh. If your seats are 12" or 14" wide, your seat back will be set at about a 15 degree angle to the seat surface and about 4" to 6" above it. You will need to measure the actual seat locations to suit the person or child that might sit in the sleigh.

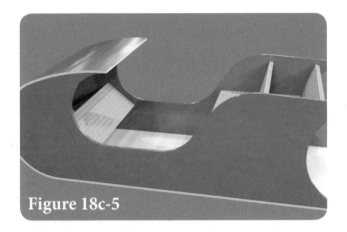

Figure 18c-5

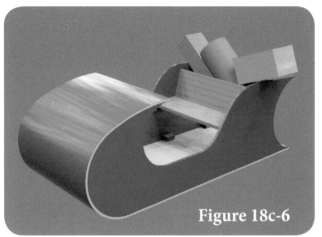

Figure 18c-6

STEP ❾

Install the footrest, seats, and seatbacks. If you plan to take the sleigh apart for storage, simply screw the boards to the cleats. Otherwise, glue and screw the boards to the cleats as shown in Figure 18c-4 and 18c-5. One or two triangular plywood braces or cleats set transversely to the sides will help to stabilize the sleigh.

STEP ❿

Paint and finish your sleigh in bright holiday colors and build a few boxes to put in the rear to make it look as if Santa is coming to town.

PROJECT 19: MAKING A PERGOLA

In my garden, a pergola does double duty. It serves to hold the grape vines, but it also covers the compost bins, making an unsightly area less messy. Pergolas enhance any yard or garden and are not very difficult to build. This project describes building an 8' x 8' square pergola. The skills that you learn from building this project will prepare you to build the gazebo in Project 25.

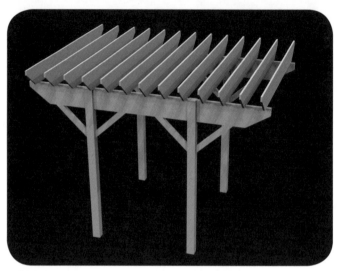

Old-time family grape growers often trained their vines on a pergola, where they would give some shade as well as make it easier to pick the fruit.

⚒ TOOLS

» Post-hole digger or good spade
» Screwdriver or hammer
» Saw, either hand or rotary
» Builder's square
» Tape measure

Figure 19-1

⟍ MATERIALS

- » Four 4" x 4" x 10' corner posts
- » Two 2" x 8" x 10' boards for support beams
- » Ten 2" x 8" x 10' boards for rafters
- » Eight 2" x 4" x 24" boards for angle braces
- » Twenty steel angle brackets to hold cross beams in place

FASTENERS:

- » Either 16P nails or 3" galvanized or ceramic-coated exterior screws for the main framing
- » 1-1/2" #8 galvanized exterior screws for the brackets

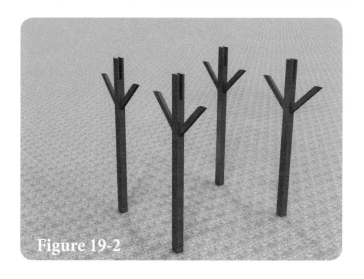

Figure 19-2

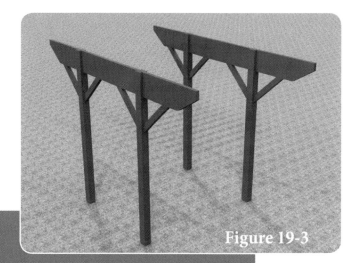

Figure 19-3

⏲ TIME *Two to 3 days*

✋ METHOD

STEP ❶

Figure 19-1 shows an exploded view of the pergola to help get the parts in the right place. Cut lap joints at the top of each post to hold the two support beams. (Figure 19-2 shows slots cut for the support beams, but since these are difficult to cut, I recommend lap joints.)

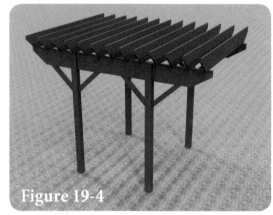
Figure 19-4

STEP ❷

Dig 2'-deep holes for the posts 8' apart in a square configuration. Set posts and check the diagonals from post to post to ensure that they are square. (Space your posts no more than 8' apart. Thus, if you are building a 16' long pergola, you will need three posts per side.)

STEP ❸

Cut a 45-degree angle on the end of each 2" x 8" x 10' support beam. Measure up 5" and across 5" to get a 45-degree angle. Set the support beams in place and screw them to the posts as shown in Figure 19-3.

STEP ❹

After cutting the ends on a 45-degree angle, attach the 2" x 4" x 24" angle braces to the posts and the support beams, as shown in Figure 19-3. (I prefer to screw the diagonal braces to the posts before setting the posts in the ground, but either method is acceptable.) These braces will help to prevent the pergola from racking in strong winds.

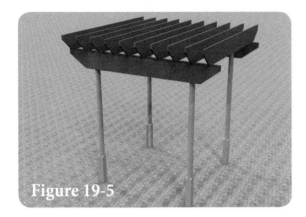

Figure 19-5

STEP ❺

Attach the rafters. Cut a 45-degree angle on the ends of each of the rafters. Set metal angle brackets on the top of each support beam at 16" on center between rafters. (The figures show a closer spacing, but stick to the 16" indicated for best results.) Set the rafters into the brackets and screw the rafters to the support beams as shown in Figure 19-4. Figure 19-5 shows the same pergola at this stage, but it has round posts instead of square. If you use round posts (available from many hardware or wood retailers), you will need to cut a flat surface at the top to bolt the support beams to. Otherwise construction is exactly the same as using square posts.

Figure 19-6

STEP ❻

Plant grape vines at each corner of the pergola. You can paint or stain the pergola, but many people prefer the look of natural wood.

⤴ OPTION 1

Setting Your Pergola on Concrete Posts

Because wood eventually rots, many builders prefer to put pergola posts on concrete support posts. Sonotubes are handy cardboard concrete forms that make setting posts easy. This small 8' x 8' square pergola only requires 8" diameter tubes. For a larger pergola with a deck, you might use a 12"-diameter tube. When constructing your pergola, the support posts will only need to be 8' tall, as they will sit on top of the concrete posts.

MATERIALS

» Four 8"-diameter Sonotubes

» Quikrete or other concrete mix (pre-mixed or dry)

» U-shaped metal brackets (to set into concrete to hold posts)

METHOD

Step 1: Dig your post-holes to a depth below the frost line (around 3' to 4' deep in most places.) and insert a Sonotube in each hole. Cut your tubes at the same height to ensure that the concrete posts will all be the same height. Make sure each tube is level. Then fill around the tubes and firmly pack the soil down.

Step 2: If using dry concrete, mix it in a wheelbarrow or cement mixer according to the manufacturer's instructions.

Step 3: Shovel or pour mixture into the tubes. Let the concrete harden for three days or more, depending upon the weather. After it has firmed up but while it is still wet, set the metal brackets in place.

Step 4: Strip off the cardboard tubes to ground level, leaving a round concrete post. Build your pergola atop the posts.

⤴ OPTION 2

Including a Deck

A deck under your pergola adds a nice touch. Here we use 1" x 6" standard decking spaced 16" apart, but you can also use cedar or other material, such as newer types of plastic composite decking (which is made from recycled materials). Check the positioning of joists if you use composite decking. Some require a 12" joist spacing.

MATERIALS

» Nine 2" x 8" x 8' boards for deck joists
» Fourteen metal joist hangers
» Sixteen 1" x 6" x 8' decking planks
» 1-1/2" galvanized nails (to fasten the joist hangers)
» Twelve 3" ceramic-coated or galvanized deck screws (to fasten the decking to the joists, three screws on each joist)

METHOD

Step 1: Screw or nail the four perimeter joists to the posts. (If you have decided to set your pergola on concrete posts, put the deck beams on metal supports on the concrete posts for added stability.)

Step 2: Nail or screw joist hangers 16" on center on two opposite deck joists. Set all the deck joists in the joist hangers and screw or nail them into place.

Step 3: Lay your decking and screw it into place as shown in Figure 19-6.

Step 4: Paint or stain the deck as desired. (Composite decking requires no treatment.)

TIME *4 to 6 hours*

A privacy screen can serve as an attractive method of hiding unsightly items such as air-conditioner units or trash cans.

This project describes how to build a free-standing screen of four separate panels, as shown in Figure 20-1. I recommend making each panel separately to allow them to be removed easily should any get damaged. Each panel is then screwed or nailed to the corner posts, with one panel being hinged to allow access. If the screen is to be placed against a house or garage, one panel can be dispensed with.

Once you have made your screen, plants are a good way to make the area more attractive. Vining plants are often a good choice, but since most drop their leaves in fall, you end up seeing the screen all winter. If you find the screen pleasing enough on its own, you can simply plant annual flowers such as nasturtiums around the screen for color accent. If you don't want to ever see the screen, evergreen plants such as yew or box will hide it completely after a few years' growth.

There are often items in your yard that, if you had the choice, you would prefer to remain unseen, such as garbage bins, garden rain barrels, and gas or heating oil tanks. A simple screen can easily be constructed to hide these items. This screen project features a lattice covering, but you can also use a bamboo screen covering or you can make the screen sides solid to completely hide the object inside.

↗ TOOLS

- » Hand saw
- » Table saw
- » Tape measure
- » Framing square
- » Hammer or screwdriver
- » Post-hole digger or spade

↘ MATERIALS

NEEDED PER PANEL:

- » Four 2" x 4" x 4' boards
- » One 4' x 4' lattice panel
- » Eight 1" x 1" x 4' trim boards (only if you do not have a table saw capable of cutting a 1/2" dado in the 2" x 4" x 4' boards)
- » Epoxy or an all-weather glue such as Gorilla Glue for the trim
- » Two exterior-grade metal hinges

FASTENERS:

- » 2" galvanized or ceramic-coated exterior screws for the panel frame
- » 2" #6 galvanized finish nails for the 1"x1" trim
- » One hook-and-eye fastener (or other preferred type of closure) for the hinged panel

⏰ TIME

About 1 to 2 hours to build each panel, and 2 to 3 hours to install the screen.

✋ METHOD

STEP ❶

Measure the space around the object you wish to screen and decide how large your screen panels need to be. Lattice panels come as large as 4' x 8', but it is easier to work with smaller panels (even if that means making up on long side of your screen out of more than one smaller panels). For this project, our screen will be composed of four panels, each 4' high by 4' wide (half a sheet of lattice for each screen).

STEP ❷

Cut a lap joint on the ends of four 2"x 4" x 4' boards.

STEP ❸

Create the groove for the lattice. If possible, run each piece through your table saw to cut a 1/2" dado or groove on the inside narrow face 3/4" deep. If you do not have a table saw, glue and screw or glue and nail the 1" x 1" x 4' trim boards exactly 1/2" apart on the inside narrow face.

STEP ❹

Cut your lattice to fit. If you're using the dado method, remove 1-1/2" on two adjacent sides, resulting in a 3' 10-1/2"-square lattice panel. If you're using the 1" x 1" x 4' trim boards to make your groove, cut off a total of 3" from any two adjacent sides, resulting in a 3' 9"-square lattice panel. This allows it to fit inside the rectangle formed by the lumber frame. Make up all four frames.

STEP ❺

Slide the cut lattice panel into the grooved frame. Screw the remaining 2"x 4" board in place to complete the panel.

Repeat Steps 1 to 4 for the next three panels.

STEP ❻

Carefully measure each frame and mark the post locations around the item that you plan to hide. Check the diagonals to ensure your screen is square. You can also screw a post on each side of one of the screen panels to ensure they are aligned properly when you dig the post holes.

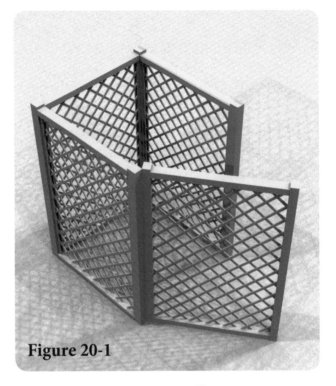

Figure 20-1

STEP ❼

Dig your post holes and set the posts into place. Before the posts are tamped down, you might want to install the screen panels, and the hinged screen panel. With everything in place, tamp the soil down firmly, check that the gate opens smoothly, and call it done.

PROJECT 21: AN A-FRAME GREENHOUSE

This simple greenhouse design measures 10' on the diagonal face, 16' long, 8' wide at the base, and 8' tall at the peak. It has a large floor for maximizing your growing area, and the A-frame sheds winter snow easily. In addition to these advantages, the greenhouse can be built so that its sidewall is oriented at about 90 degrees to the sun, putting the most solar energy into heating the greenhouse instead of being reflected away. Triangular window vents in the ends of the greenhouse allow cool air to flow in under the glazing on each side when the temperature gets too hot. This greenhouse frame is made of 2" x 8" x 12' joists and covered with 4' x 10' sheets of polycarbonate glazing. The glazing is available in a variety of thicknesses, from 6 mm up to 16 mm, depending on your location and climate. Thicker glazing will keep it warmer in the winter; this a better alternative for northern latitudes.

MATERIALS

» Six 6" x 6" x 8' (or 8" x 8" x 8') ground contact lumber for the foundation buried to slightly more than half its depth

» Four 2" x 4" x 8' boards (two for the vertical end wall studs; two for the end sill plates)

» Four 2" x 4" x 10' boards for the diagonal end wall studs

» One 2" x 6" x 4' board for the header above the door

» One 2" x 10" x 16' board for the ridge pole. (Select top-quality lumber with grain running from end to end, if possible.)

» Ten 2" x 6" x 12' boards for the rafters

» Two 2" x 4" x 16' boards for the side sill plates

This simple greenhouse design allows you to grow taller plants, such as tomato, near the middle and smaller plants, such as lettuce, near the edges.

» Eight 4' x 10' polycarbonate glazing sheets

» Six 10' long H sections (The glazing slides into the top and bottom of the H, which is set on its side to form a watertight joint.)

» Two 4' x 8' polycarbonate glazing sheets for the ends

» Four 1"x 10" x 8' boards for side bottom vents (to be placed along the bottom edge of the glazing)

» Twelve 2" hinges for the side vents

» Four 1" x 4" x 8' boards to set above the opening boards to fasten the hinges to

» Two 1" x 6" x 16' or four 1" x 6" x 8' boards to be used as trim to cover the ridge and make it watertight. (You might also look at one of the far more durable engineered wood products for the ridge trim. I have found that it lasts a lot longer, but does have a tendency to collect algae and turn a little green.)

» Six 2" x 6" x 2' boards for the end vents

» Four 2" hinges for the end vents

» One 3' wide 6' 6" door

» Two hinges

» One handle

FASTENERS:

» 6" or 8" TimberLOK screws for the foundation

» Either 16P nails or 3" galvanized or ceramic-coated exterior screws to fasten the joists to the ridge pole and to frame out the end wall

» 1-1/2" #8 or #10 screws to secure the glazing

» 2" or 3" #6 or #8 galvanized or ceramic-coated nails for the covering boards at the ridge

» Caulking for the ridge pieces

⚒ TOOLS

- » Hand or rotary saw
- » Tape measure
- » Screwdriver or hammer

- » Electric drill with oversize hole bit (to drill the polycarbonate when installing the glazing)

✋ METHOD

STEP ❶

Lay out your foundation by marking the corners and checking that your diagonals are equal. Dig a trench and install your 6" x 6" lumber around the perimeter. (If your garden suffers from burrowing rodents, I suggest you dig down 24" to 30" inches and bury chicken wire vertically around the perimeter to prevent rodents from tunneling under the foundation, entering the greenhouse, and eating your produce. Staple the chicken wire to the foundation.)

🕐 TIME *Thirty to 40 hours*

STEP ❷

Frame the ends. For the non-door end, use three 2" x 4" lumber studs to support the ridge pole. Cut the 2" x 4" x 8' center stud down by 10" to accommodate the width of the ridge pole. Cut the 2" x 4" x 10' diagonal outer studs to suit the rafter slope. Temporarily screw a 2 x 4 brace across the top of the three studs to hold them in place until the ridge pole is fastened to the two end walls. Figure 21-1 shows the layout for the end wall with a door.

For the door end, cut the 2" x 4" x 10' diagonal outer studs exactly as was done for the other end wall. a stud on either side of the door and a header to go over the door. Set the two 2" x 4" x 8' door studs and the 2" x 6" x 4' header to accommodate the 3' wide door. Cut the ends of the stud and the header on a 65 degree angle. Screw or nail in place. You will also need three pieces of scrap 2"x4" to form a support for the ridge pole on top of the door header.

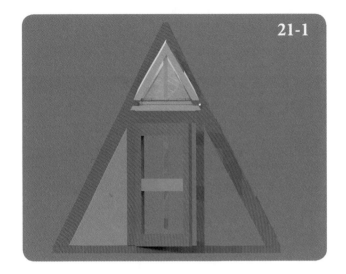

21-1

STEP ❸

Set up both ends of the greenhouse on the foundation and brace them into position.

STEP ❹

Install the ridge pole and screw or nail it into position.

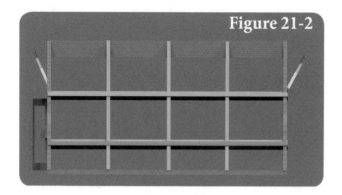

Figure 21-2

STEP 5

Install the side rafters. The ends of the rafters will need to be cut to suit the angle of the foundation and the ridge pole. Rafter spacing is 4' or to suit the width of the polycarbonate that you are planning to use. Figure 21-2 shows the side view and rafter spacing. Screw or toenail the rafters to the sill plate and foundation at the bottom. Measure halfway up the rafters and screw or nail the glazing brace in place. The frame is complete as shown in Figure 21-3.

STEP 6

Install the bottom side vents. (If you are not going to paint the greenhouse leave the vents off until you install the glazing, as shown in Figure 21-4.) Using four pieces of 1" x 10" x 8' as opposed to two 16' boards allows you more control over the amount of venting you use. Fasten the vents to the joists with the hinges.

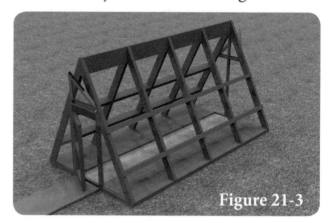

Figure 21-3

STEP 7

Paint or stain the woodwork, if that is your intention.

OPTIONS

If you wish you can insulate one end or put doors in both ends. You can also lengthen the greenhouse by adding bays in 4' increments.

STEP 8

Install the plastic 'H' shaped sealing pieces by screwing them horizontally to the rafters.

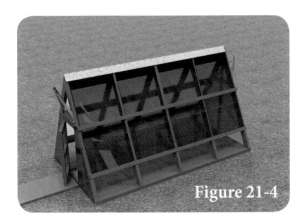

Figure 21-4

STEP 9

Install the glazing. Make sure to leave a 6" gap at the bottom as shown in Figure 21-4. The glazing should be pressed tightly together at the top. You will need to drill oversized holes for the glazing to allow for it to expand and shrink. The distances will depend on the thickness of the glazing that you are using. You should also use 'H' pieces between the glazing to ensure a good watertight joint.

STEP 10

Seal the top. Screw the 1" x 6" lumber to the ridge pole. Countersink the screws and putty over them. Remember to caulk between the two pieces on either side of the ridge to ensure it stays watertight.

STEP 11

Build the triangular vents for the ends. Cut scraps of glazing to fit and attach. By hinging these triangular vents at the bottom, they naturally fall open and are easily adapted for automatic window openers. That said, you can hinge the vents on one side instead of the bottom if you wish.

STEP 12

Install the door and bring your plants into the comfort of their new home.

PROJECT 22: ADIRONDACK CHAIR

The Adirondack chair is renowned for its comfort, but the name Adirondack is a misnomer. They were never manufactured in the Adirondack mountains, nor are they normally made from trees grown there. Most authorities agree that the chair known today as the Adirondack originated around the turn of the twentieth century and was based upon the design of the Westport chair. The Westport got its name from the town of Westport, New York, which is located near Lake Champlain, about ten miles east of the Adirondack range. The Westport chair differed from the Adirondack mainly in that it had wide, solid pieces of lumber for the seat and backrest (as we show in the optional chair). In all probability, as 15"- to 18"-wide boards of lumber became scarce, it was more practical and less expensive to use thinner boards for this type of chair.

This trend gave the Adirondack chair the slatted look that we know today. It also made repairs much easier. Repairing the seat or back of a Westport chair meant replacing a major portion of the chair. In contrast, repairing an Adirondack is a matter of replacing a slat or two.

A patent for the Westport chair was applied for in 1904 by a Harry Bunnell who, it is said, got the basic design from Thomas Lee. Since that time, there have been many different variations. Seat heights vary considerably, as does the seat back angle. Besides the classic Adirondack chair for one adult there are matching children's versions, rocking chair versions, bench seat versions, love seat versions, as well as foot stools and tables. Some of these are illustrated in the following projects.

 TIME   *Three to 4 hours*

Lean back in this chair and enjoy the fruits of your labors.

⚒ TOOLS

- » Jigsaw, sabre saw, or hand saw
- » Compass for marking curved armrest and back tops
- » Builder's square
- » Pencil
- » Electric drill with #40 bit for wood screws and countersink bit
- » Ruler or measuring tape
- » Putty knife
- » Sandpaper (various grades)
- » Oil-based paint (primer and topcoat in the desired color) or stain
- » Wood putty

OPTIONAL TOOLS

- » Plane
- » Spokeshave

MATERIALS

Wood:

» No. 1 Grade common pine

» Note: In America, 1" x 4" lumber measures approximately 3/4" x 3 1/2".

For the seat base:

» Six 1" x 4" x 22" boards for the seat bottom and front

» One 1" x 2" x 22" board for the back support

» Two 1" x 4" x 20-1/4" boards for the front legs

» Two 1" x 4" x 42" boards for the seat supports

» Two 1" x 2" x 6" boards, cut as shown for the arm support

For the Seat Back:

» Two 1" x 4" x 40" long boards for the center pieces

» Two 1" x 4" x 38" boards for next to center pieces

» Two 1" x 4" x 40" long boards for the outer pieces.

» One 1" x 2" x 22" board for bottom back panel cross brace

» One 1" x 2" x 20-1/2" board for top back panel cross brace

For the arm-rests:

» Two 1" x 6" x 27" boards for arm rests with ends rounded and inside faces curved

» One 1-1/2" x 1-1/2" x 26" board for the arm support

Fasteners:

» One box 1-1/4" #8 Phillips head wood screws (Note that all screws should be countersunk and the heads puttied over (the nicer chairs have wooden plugs to cover the screws) to a smooth finish.)

» Waterproof glue

✋ METHOD

Figure 22-1

The chair is made of three sub-assemblies: the seatback, the seat, and the armrest. Each part takes less than an hour to build and the entire project should take three to four hours. To enable you to see how all the parts fit together, an exploded view of the chair is shown in Figure 22-1.

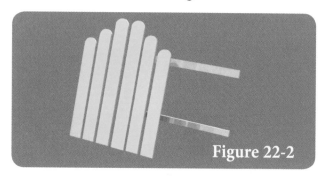

Figure 22-2

STEP ❶

Build the seat back. Mark out the pieces for the seatback. Radius the top of each piece or cut it to your desired shape.

Cut the cross braces to length and position the parts of the seatback on them 1/8" apart. Make sure the bottom brace is aligned one and a half inches up from the bottom, since it will be resting on the seat section. The top brace should be positioned slightly up from the bottom brace. (Note that the bottom brace is 22" long, and the top brace is only 20-1/2" long.) Drill countersink holes and screw the seatback parts to the cross braces to complete the seatback. Figure 22-2 shows the seat back.

STEP ❷

Build the seat base: Shape the seat supports. Draw in the slight curvature of the seat along the top of each support. The recess is about 18" long and 1/2" deep at its deepest point. Lay out the curve by holding a thin batten trim piece at the deepest part of the seat and at the ends, then flexing it to curve it to the 1/2" depth. Have a helper draw the curve. Cut the curve out with a sabre saw and use a spokeshave to smooth it out. (If you do not have a spokeshave, sand out the worst cut marks and cover the rest with the seat.)

At the front of the seat draw a 3" radius on the top corner of the support. Similarly, at the other end of the support draw a 3" radius on the top corner of the support. Mark the height of the front support on the front leg (the seat height will be 16" at the front) and insert a single screw to hold the seat support to the front leg. Take a

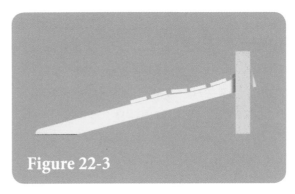

Figure 22-3

long straight edge and mark from the foot of the front support to the trailing edge of the seat support. Cut off the excess to get a tapered leg as shown in Figure 22-3. Screw and glue the front leg to the seat support.

Drill countersink holes in all the slats of the seat and screw them to the seat support. Make sure to leave 1/8" between each slat. You will need to round off the front of the seat to ensure the transverse slats are well rounded. Sharp edges will be uncomfortable for the back of your knees!

METHOD

STEP ❸

Add the armrest supports. Figure 22-4a shows the seat assembled and ready for the back. (You can insert the back into the seat base as shown in Figure 22-4b to make sure everything fits, but the seat back will not stay in place without the armrest.)

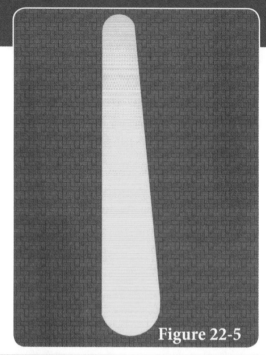

Figure 22-5

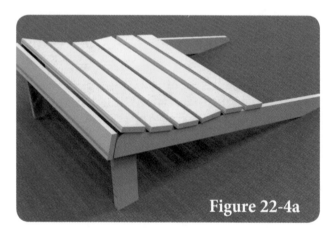

Figure 22-4a

Figure 22-4b

Figure 22-6

STEP ❹

Making the armrests. Mark out the armrests as shown in Figure 22-5 and cut them to shape with a 6" radius on the large end and a 3" radius on the small end. You may want to plane the cuts and sand the rounded corners to a smooth finish. Drill two countersink holes and screw the armrests to the cross brace as shown in Figure 22-6.

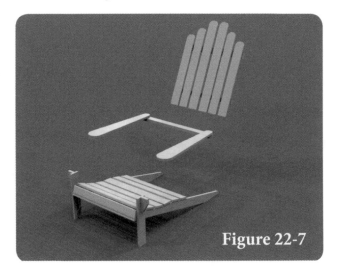

Figure 22-7

STEP ❺

Drill two countersink holes through the armrests into the armrest supports on the front legs. Glued and screw the pieces together. *Do not put downward pressure on the back of the armrest at this stage.* Figure 22-7 shows the three major assemblies of the chair ready to be joined.

Now carefully slide the assembled seatback into position between the last seat slat and the seat back support slat. To secure the seatback, you can either screw through it to the armrest crossbrace or add another crossbrace immediately under the armrest crossbrace. I prefer to secure the entire chair together by screwing the seatback to the armrest crossbrace.

STEP ❻

Fill all the screw holes with putty, brush paint any knots with a sealer, and paint the entire chair with a coat of oil-based primer. Follow this with a coat of undercoat and two coats of high-gloss exterior topcoat. Sand the chair lightly between coats. Alternatively, you can apply stain.

⚑ OPTIONS

A similar construction method can be employed to make a narrowback Westport-style chair as shown in Figure 22-8. This chair uses a single wide plank (probably hard to find today and you may have to resort to edge-gluing two or three planks together.) for the back with the rest of the chair constructed as for the Adirondack chair. Figure 22-9 shows an exploded view of this chair.

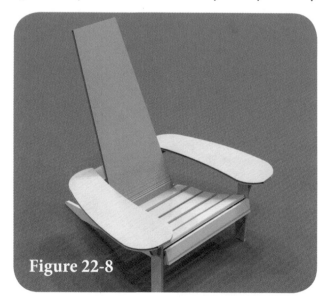

Figure 22-8

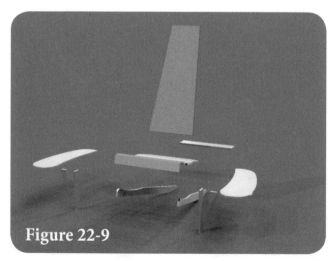

Figure 22-9

PROJECT 23: AN ADIRONDACK-STYLE TABLE AND FOOTREST

To match the Adirondack chair that you made in the last project, you can also make a comfortable footrest and a small side table. This table is 3' long, but you can scale it up or down and set it between two Adirondack chairs to hold a summer's worth of books, suntan lotion, pretzels, and lemonade. The sloped design of the legs makes the table more stable.

The footrest is the same height as the chair and butts directly against it, making for an even more comfortable sitting experience. Like the chair, it is relatively easy to construct and should take no more than an hour or two.

⏲ TIME *2–4 hours*

Make an attractive deck or outdoor furniture set by adding a table and footrest to your Adirondack chair project.

↗ TOOLS

- » Jigsaw, sabre saw, or hand saw
- » Compass for marking curved board ends
- » Builder's square
- » Pencil
- » Electric drill with #40 bit for wood screws
- » Countersink bit
- » Ruler or measuring tape
- » Putty knife
- » Sandpaper (various grades)
- » Oil-based paint (primer and topcoat in the desired color) or stain
- » Wood putty

OPTIONAL TOOLS

- » Plane

↖ MATERIALS

- » No. 1 Grade common pine
- » Two 1" x 4" x 36" boards for center panels
- » Two 1" x 4" x 34" boards for next to center panels
- » Two 1" x 4" x 32" boards for outer panels
- » Three 1" x 4" x 22" or 2" x 2" x 24" boards for table supports
- » Four 2" x 2" x 24" boards for legs (If you wish to make a lower table, use 18" legs.)
- » Two 1" x 2" x 24" boards for cross braces to support legs
- » Two 1" x 4" x 36" boards for cross braces to support the table lengthwise

FASTENERS:

- » One box 1-1/4" #8 wood screws

✋ METHOD

❋ BUILDING THE TABLE ❋

STEP ❶

Make the tabletop first. Radius the top of each piece using your compass and saw, as shown in Figure 23-1. Set the table support pieces on a flat surface and countersink drill and screw the table top panels to them. Use two screws at each join.

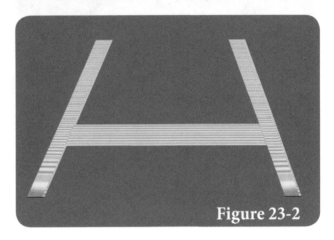

Figure 23-2

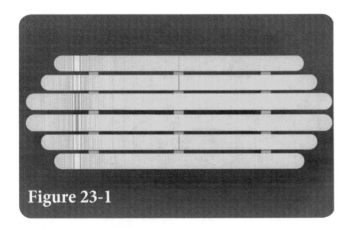

Figure 23-1

STEP ❷

Make the legs. Space the top of the legs 18" apart then lap-join the 22" brace to the legs 6" up from the bottom of the leg, as shown in Figure 23-2.

STEP ❸

Connect the legs to the tabletop. Turn the tabletop over and screw the legs to the table top.

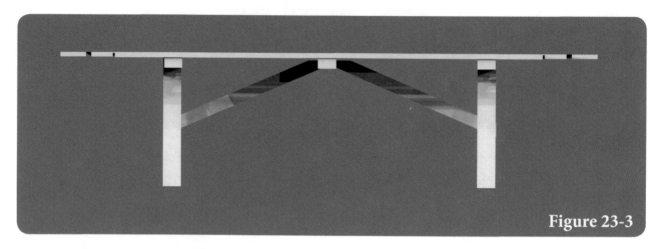

Figure 23-3

STEP ❹

Measure and cut the lengthwise braces. (They are to be positioned on the centerline to stop the table racking fore and aft.) They will be attached to the center-point of the leg braces using a lap joint. Cut the opposite ends on an angle to suit their connection to the underside of the tabletop. (You can skip these braces, but experience has shown that somebody will put a foot on the end of the table and it will collapse without them!) Figure 23-3 shows the table with the cross braces. Figure 24-4 shows an exploded view of the table showing how the parts go together.

STEP ❺

Paint or stain the table to match the chairs you made in Project 22.

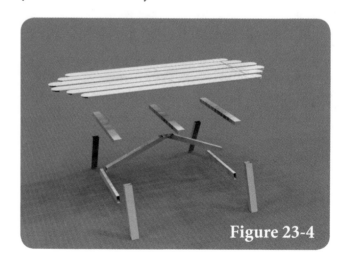

Figure 23-4

✸ MAKING THE FOOTREST ✸

🕐 TIME

About 2 hours, plus more time for painting

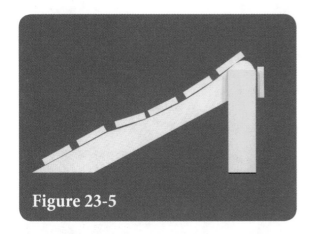

Figure 23-5

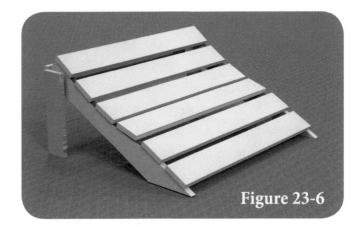

Figure 23-6

↘ MATERIALS

» Two 1" x 4" x 20" boards for the supports (Try different lengths to make the leg rest slope just the way you prefer.)

» Two 1" x 4" x 16" boards for the legs

» Seven 1" x 4" x 18" boards for the slats (Use the same-sized and type material as you used for the chair to ensure they match.)

FASTENERS:

» 1-1/4" #8 Phillips-head wood screws or 2" #10 Phillips-head wood screws

METHOD

STEP ❶

Put a single screw in the vertical post and the sloping support. Adjust the slope of the leg to one that you prefer. Cut the sloping supports to shape like you did for the Adirondack chair and as shown if Figure 23-5. The depth of cut should be no more than 1/2" over a 12" to 15" curve. When you are satisfied with the curvature of the footrest screw and glue the leg and supports together.

STEP ❷

Screw the slats to the supports using two screws at each end of each slat. One slat is attached to the top back of the footrest, as shown in Figure 23-5. Check that the leg rest is comfortable. Sand or radius the top slat to remove the sharp top edge. Figure 23-6 shows an exploded view of the footrest.

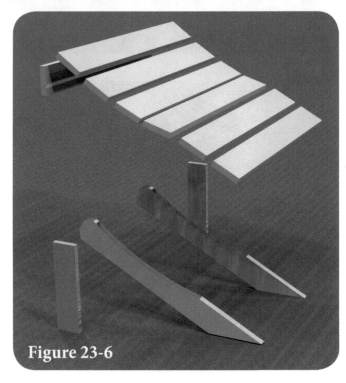

Figure 23-6

STEP ❸

Paint or stain the table to match the chairs you made in Project 22.

166

PROJECT 24: A RECLINER FOR YOUR DECK OR PATIO

A recliner takes the Adirondack chair concept a little further, making a comfortable lounging chair for enjoying the day poolside, on the patio, or in the garden.

There is nothing quite like being able to stretch out on a recliner in full sunshine on a Sunday afternoon knowing that you have absolutely nothing else to do. This recliner is made using materials to match the previous two projects and will complement your entire Adirondack set. It is designed to allow the back to be adjusted to almost any height, and can be fitted with an armrest or with rollers to enable it to be moved anywhere.

It works best if you have a two-part (3" or 4" thick) outdoor cushion set made to fit the chair. One part of the cushion should be sized to fit the lower portion of the recliner, while the upper portion of the cushion should be made to fit the back so that it can be adjusted as desired.

⏰ TIME
4–6 hours plus time to paint or stain the recliner

⟋ TOOLS

- » Jigsaw, sabre saw, or hand saw
- » Compass for marking curved back tops
- » Builder's square
- » Pencil
- » Electric drill with #40 bit for wood screws
- » Countersink bit
- » Ruler or measuring tape

- » Putty knife
- » Sandpaper (various grades)
- » Oil-based paint (primer and topcoat in the desired color) or stain
- » Wood putty

OPTIONAL TOOLS

- » Plane

↖ MATERIALS

For the Base:

» Two 2" x 6" x 72" boards for the base supports

» Fourteen 1" x 4" x 22" boards for the bed slats

» Four 1" x 4" x 12" boards for the legs

» Four 1" x 4" x 15" boards for the leg braces

For the Seat Back

» One 1" x 3" x 40" board for the center back panel

» Two 1" x 3" x 38" boards– for next-to-center pieces

» Two 1" x 3" x 36" boards for the next outer pieces

» Two 1" x 3" x 34" boards for outer pieces of back

» Two 1" x 2" x 22" boards for cross braces to hold the back panels together

For the Back Adjustment Assembly:

» One 1" x 24" dowel

» Two 1" x 2" x 15" boards for the dowel support for back adjustment

» Four 1" x 4" scrap pieces, 4" on the bottom, 3" at the top, drilled on center for the 1" dowel. These pieces are screwed and glued to the seatback on each side of the dowel support boards.

» Two 3"x 3/8" bolts (with nuts and washers), to hold the dowel support arms to the scrap pieces above. You can also use a 3/8" x 24" metal rod across the seat back.

» One 1/2" x 24" metal bar for the back to pivot on

Fasteners:

» One box 1-1/4" #8 wood screws

» Waterproof glue

✋ METHOD

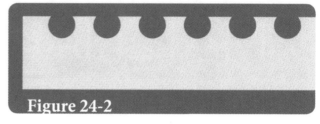

Figure 24-2

Figure 24-1

STEP ❶

To build the base, clamp the two 72"-long base supports together and cut the notches for the seat back dowel to rest in. The best way to do this is to clamp a piece of scrap 2" x 4" wood to the top of the base supports, as shown in Figure 24-1, and drill holes through both the scrap wood and the base support wood. Figure 24-2 shows the scrap wood removed. Trim off the front corners of all the holes, as shown in Figure 24-3.

Next, build the bed. Place the base supports on a flat surface spaced 22" apart. Drill two countersink holes for each join, then glue and screw the bed slats to the base supports, leaving a small space about 1/8" between each slat. Attach

two slats to the front of the base. One slat will be across the end of the 72" long base support. A second slat will be installed on the front legs, 4" up from the bottom of the legs. Figure 24-4 shows the basic bed without the legs.

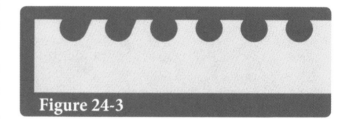

Figure 24-3

Note that the leg at the bottom of the bed is at the end of the base support, and the leg at the head end of the bed is 6" or 8" in from the end to give maximum support to the backrest support.

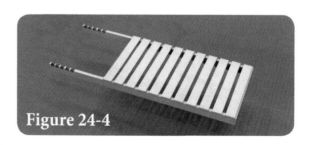

Figure 24-4

Figure 24-5

STEP ❷

Mark out the pieces for the seat back. Radius the top of each piece or cut it to your desired shape. Cut the cross braces to length and position the parts of the seat back on them 1/8" apart. The bottom brace should be flush with the bottom of the seat back slats. The top brace should be positioned 24 up from the bottom brace. Drill countersink holes and screw the seatback parts to the cross braces, as shown in Figure 24-6. (Tops may be rounded or decorated in some other fashion.)

Figure 24-6

STEP ❸

The seat back assembly can be made in one of two ways. The first step is to make the bottom assembly. If you use a bottom brace made of the 3" x 3" x 22" piece, you will need to drill a 1/2" hole through the center. This will require a drill bit at least 12" long and some very careful drilling. Or you can make a box using two 1" x 2" x 22" and two 1" x 3/4" x 22" boards through which the 1/2" diameter metal rod passes.

To make the box, glue and screw the 3/4" x 3/4" pieces to the edges of the 1" x 2" pieces and push the rod through the middle.

When you have made this box or drilled the hole, glue and screw the assembly to the bottom of the seat back slats. Space The seat back slats about 1/8" to 1/4" so that they take up about 21 1/2" of the 22" available.

Set the upper cross brace 24" above the bottom box brace and glue and screw the slats to it.

Under the upper cross brace on the outermost slats, Glue and screw the 1" x 4" tapered scrap pieces 3/4" apart. The upper end of the back support assembly should fit between these pieces.

STEP ❹

To make the back support assembly, take the two 1" x 2" x 15" boards and round off both ends using a 3/4" radius. At the center of the radius drill a 1" diameter hole at one end and a 3/8" hole at the other end. Insert the 1" dowel through the 1" diameter hole and glue it in place. Bolt the back support assembly to the seat back.

Figure 24-7

STEP ❺

Set the backrest in place on the base, as in Figure 24-7.

STEP ❻

Paint or stain the recliner to match the rest of your Adirondack collection.

OPTIONS

✷ ADDING AN ARMREST ✷

» One 1" x 6" x 27" board for armrest

» Two 1-1/2" x 1-1/2" x 16" boards for armrest supports

» Four 1/4" x 4" bolts, washers, and nuts

Figure 24-8

STEP 1

Attach supports. The rearmost support is set against the next to last seat slat (one slat from the back rest). The second support is placed four slats nearer the foot of the bed or approximately 16". Drill two 1/4" holes through each support and the base. Attach with bolts.

STEP 2

Radius the ends of the armrest. If desired, round out the inside face of the armrest. Drill countersink holes through the armrest into the supports, then glue and screw in place. Figure 24-8 shows the recliner with the armrest.

OPTIONS

✹ ADDING WHEELS ✹

If you wish to add wheels to the head end of the recliner, shorten the legs and drill them for 1/2" steel axle. If you use 6" diameter wheels, shorten the legs by about 4". Larger diameter wheels will require removal of more leg. The axle should go entirely across the recliner to serve both wheels and to ensure they remain square when rolling the bed. Figure 24-9 shows the recliner with wheels.

Figure 24-9

If you don't have a place to put your Adirondack chair or recliner, build this gazebo to make sure that you can enjoy all your projects.

⏰ TIME

This project might take 2–3 weeks, depending on the help available. You will need a partner to help move joists and heavy sheets of plywood. In total, it will probably take around 60 to 80 hours for two workers, not including painting.

Imagine it's an August Sunday afternoon, and you need a cool place to get out of the hot sun; a place to relax and read the paper; a place where you can sling a hammock if you want to, or lie out on the recliner you built in Project 24, or set out the table you built in Project 23. There are so many things you can do when you are in this gazebo.

The project is not difficult when it is broken down into several parts. It will, however, take several weekends to build, but think

of the number of weekends that you are going to spend enjoying it. Because this is a fairly large permanent structure, 10 feet by 16 feet, you might have to apply for a permit in your area, or you might have to adhere to local building codes. Do not erect the gazebo without anchoring it down. In high winds it may be moved or may even tip over.

You can adjust these instructions to make a larger or smaller gazebo to suit your space. Because there are so many ways to build and finish the gazebo, several options have been outlined in the text.

TOOLS

- » Jigsaw, sabre saw, or hand saw
- » Builder's square
- » Pencil
- » Electric drill with #40 bit for wood screws
- » Countersink bit
- » Ruler or measuring tape
- » Putty knife
- » Sandpaper (various grades)
- » Oil-based paint (primer and topcoat in the desired color) or stain
- » Wood putty

MATERIALS

FOR THE GROUND SURFACE:

» Enough heavy-duty plastic or cardboard to cover 160 square feet

» Enough 1/2" or 3/4" stone to cover 160 square feet with a 6" layer

» Pressure-treated wood for the base supports, the remainder can be pine.

FOR THE DECK:

» Seventeen 2" x 10" x 10' pressure-treated boards for joists, 16" on center with end joists doubled up

» Two 2" x 10" x 16' pressure-treated boards for joist caps

» Four 1/2" x 4' x 8' sheets of pressure-treated plywood for the sub floor

» Any combination of 1" x 6" decking in 8',10', 12', or 16' lengths.

» Twenty-eight metal joist hangers

FASTENERS:

» 1-1/2" galvanized nails to fasten the joist hangers

» 2" galvanized common nails to fasten the plywood to the joists

FOR THE ROOF SUPPORTS:

» Eight 4" x 4" x 10' pressure-treated posts (if you plan to set sink them into the ground) or eight 4" x 4" x 8' posts if they will be set on concrete). The exterior joists are fastened to the posts with either a lap joint or with 6" x 3/8" bolts, two per post.

» Sixteen 4" x 4" x 2' or 3' boards for the angle brackets (Use scrap lengths, if available.)

» Two 2" x 10" x 16' joists set horizontally along the long sides at the top of the posts

» Two 2" x 10" x 10' joists set horizontally along the short sides at the top of the posts

FASTENERS:

» Use either 3" galvanized or ceramic coated screws or 8P nails to fix the angle brackets to the posts.

FOR THE ROOF:

» Fourteen 2" x 8" x 10' boards for joists (four for the flat part of the roof, eight for the sloped roof, and one for each gable end)

» One 2" x 10" x 12' board for ridge pole

» Four 2" x 8" x 8' boards for side joist caps

» Two 2" x 8" x 10' boards for end joist caps

» Six 1" x 8" x 10' boards for trim (painted to the desired color)

» Twelve 1/2" x 4' x 8' plywood sheets for roof cladding

FASTENERS:

» Either 16P nails or 3" galvanized or ceramic-coated screws to fasten the roof joists to the perimeter joists. (You will need to toenail screws or nails at each "birdmouth" to fasten the joists to the perimeter joists.)

» 1-1/2" or 2" galvanized common nails to fasten the plywood to the joists

ROOF COVERING:

» If you use composite roof shingles, you will need: about 50 linear feet of drip edge (it comes in 10' lengths), one to two rolls of roofing felt, approximately 16 to 18 bundles of three tab roofing shingles, and 1-1/2" roofing nails.

FOR THE HANDRAIL (UNLESS INSTALLING THE SEATS):

» Two 2" x 4" x 16' boards

» Either 16P nails or 3" galvanized or ceramic-coated screws for fasteners.

FOR THE SEATS:

» Eight 1" x 4" x 16' boards (either cedar decking or painted pine) (Can be made of four pieces of 1" x 4".)

» Four 1" x 6" x 16' or 1" x 8" x 16' boards for seat backs

» Sixteen pieces of 1" x 6" x 20" seat supports

» Eight 2" x 4" x 26" boards for seat back supports

FASTENERS:

» Either 16P nails or 3" galvanized or ceramic-coated screws to screw the seat supports to the posts

» 2" or 2-1/2" galvanized or ceramic-coated nails or screws to fasten the seats and seatbacks to the supports

✋ METHOD

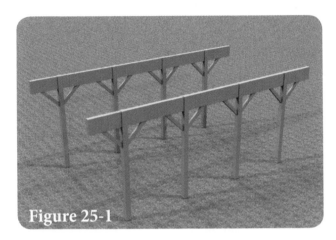

Figure 25-1

STEP ❶

Select your site and measure the area carefully, marking the location of your corners and your posts. The 4" x 4" support posts are spaced 4' apart, making the gazebo footprint 10' wide by 16' long. Check the diagonals to ensure that the gazebo is square.

STEP ❷

Install your support posts and braces. Dig your 2'-deep post-holes in the appropriate spots and set your posts in place, making sure they are all level, as shown in Figure 25-1. (If you plan on erecting the gazebo

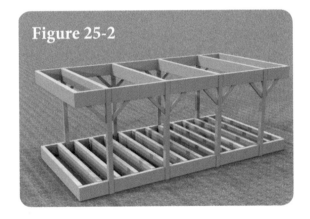

Figure 25-2

on a concrete surface, you will probably have to drill or jackhammer down a few inches and set steel plates in the concrete to hold the support posts.) Cut angles on each end of the angle brackets. Screw one brace on each side of each post.

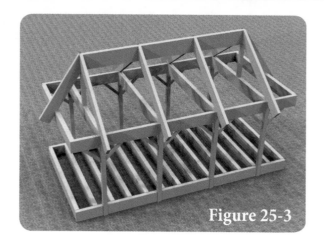

Figure 25-3

STEP ❸

Prepare the ground surface. To prevent weeds from growing up under the decking, you should cover the area with either plastic or heavy duty cardboard and pour a 6" layer of 1/2" or 3/4" stone over it.

STEP ❹

Frame the deck. Attach the end and side joists to the outside of the support posts. Install the floor joists on 16" centers. With the deck framed up and to ensure that the posts stayed square the 2" x 8" or 2" x 10" roof framework is installed as shown in Figure 25-2 and 3.

Cover the deck with the pressure treated plywood. Note how the sheets of plywood are staggered, as shown in Figure 25-4, to ensure that the joints are not all in the same place. Each joint falls on a transverse beam.

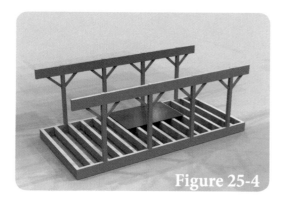

Figure 25-4

ALTERNATIVE STEP ❹

Lay the wooden decking. Install longitudinally with the joints randomly scattered.

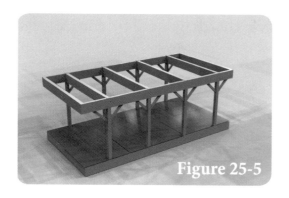

Figure 25-5

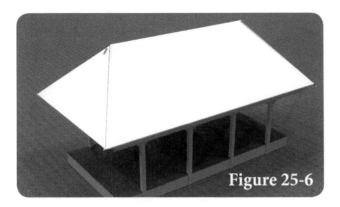

Figure 25-6

STEP ❺

Install the roof joists. The horizontal roof joists are notched into the vertical posts. To do this you will have to cut a 10" x 2" notch in the top of each post. The diagonal bracing will be fastened to the post and to the horizontal joist as shown in Figure 25-2.

Build the sloped roof. The ridge piece is set up first. To set it in place cut two pieces of 2" x 4" approximately 3' 9" long. Toenail them to a horizontal rafter 2' from the outermost rafter. Set the 2" x 10" x 12' ridge piece in place. (You may want to add temporary 2" x 4" x 8" cleats on either side of the vertical supports to hold the ridge piece in place.

The roof joists are cut with a 45 degree angle at the upper end and a birdmouth at the lower end. They are raised up, the 45 degree ends set against the ridge piece and nailed into place. The birdmouth notch rests on the horizontal joist and is toenailed into place.

The ends have a 2" x 8" x 5' 4" (approximately) rafter nailed on centerline, and a 2" x 8" x 6' 4" (approximately) nailed to the corners. The upper ends of these rafters will be cut at about a 35 degree angle; the lower ends will have a birdmouth notch.

With the rafters in place, nail 2" x 10" x 10' boards on the lower ends of the rafters all around the roof eaves. (These 2" x 10" pieces will be covered with painted 1" x 10" trim pieces.)

• Install the plywood on the roof. Lay 1/2" plywood over the sloped joists in a staggered fashion to ensure rigidity. (In this case the plywood need not be pressure treated, since it will be covered with shingles.) Note in Figure 25-6 how the gable ends are framed up with lumber cut diagonally to the apex.

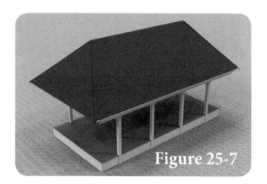

Figure 25-7

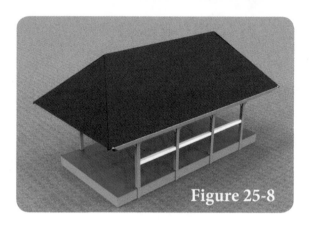

Figure 25-8

STEP 6

Lay your roof covering. With the plywood installed, as shown in Figure 25-6, you can install your roofing materials. The most conventional is to put a drip edge around the roof eaves, then cover the roof with roofing felt and nail down three-tab composite roof shingles, as in Figure 25-7. A prettier but slightly more expensive finish is to nail down red cedar shingles. In your area, you might use roof tiles or another method.

STEP 7

Install the hand rail. The least expensive finish (and one that is required if you have a drop-off on any side) is to install a hand rail around the gazebo, as shown in Figure 25-8. But a better finish might be to install seats on one, two or three sides. (See Step 7 alternate below.)

ALTERNATIVE STEP ❼

Install seats. The 16"-wide seats are located 16" above the deck level with the seat backs a further 8" or 9" (check to see what is comfortable) above the deck level, as shown in Figure 25-9.

Figure 25-9

Screw the seat support pieces on either side of the support posts. Lay the seat boards atop the seat supports, drill countersink holes, and screw in place.

Cut the seat back supports with bottom ends angle cut to suit the deck and tops cut on an angle to suit the seat back. Drill and screw the supports to the deck. Drill countersink holes and screw the seat back to the seat back supports.

STEP ❽

Over the plywood floor, you can lay tile, a second layer of painted plywood, or any waterproof flooring such as bamboo or teak decking.

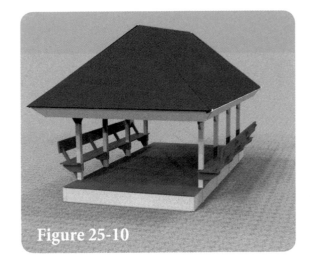

Figure 25-10